Take Five! Links for Language Arts

180 Bell-ringers That Build Critical-thinking Skills

KAYE HAGLER

Take Five! Links for Language Arts

180 Bell-ringers That Build Critical-thinking Skills

Kaye Hagler

Cover design: Studio Montage

Book design: Mariana Wallig

Library of Congress Cataloging-in-Publication Data

Hagler, Kaye R.

Take five! : links for language arts : 180 bell-ringers that build critical-thinking skills / by Kaye R. Hagler.

p. cm.

Includes bibliographical references and index.

ISBN 978-1-937412-03-6 (paperback)

1. Critical thinking--Study and teaching--Activity programs. 2. Critical thinking--Study and teaching--Audio-visual aids. 3. English language--Study and teaching--Audio-visual aids. 4. Teaching--Aids and devices. 5. Motivation in education. I. Title.

LB1590.3.H35 2011

370.15'2--dc23

2011029215

Maupin House publishes professional resources for K-12 educators. Contact us for tailored, in-school training or visit www.maupinhouse.com for free lesson plan downloads. Kaye Hagler is available to speak at conferences and to visit schools, libraries, and professional development workshops throughout North America.

Maupin House, Inc.
1710 Roe Crest Drive
Mankato, MN 56003
www.maupinhouse.com

Printed in the United States of America in Eau Claire, Wisconain.
012915 008760

Dedication

This book is dedicated to:

Tom and Kathleen Richards, my parents and lifelong educators

My son, Seth, now following his own educational path

My former students who tackled my many strange and unusual prompts

And, most importantly, to Terry— my support, my companion, my husband

Table of Contents

Part I:

Introduction

During my twenty plus years as a teacher in elementary, middle, and high school classrooms, I have tried almost every bell-ringer on the market. After all, the bell-ringer serves as a valuable classroom management tool for those crucial (and all-too-often chaotic) minutes at the beginning of the class period.

Many textbook companies pack their teacher kits with formulaic bell ringers, but just how exciting can a subject/verb agreement problem be? Few students will emit radiant beams of mental joy at the prospect of finding three capitalization errors in a sentence. And while story starters work well, there's more to cover in the language arts classroom than just narrative elements, the topic commonly chosen.

Although visual prompts can successfully engage students' attention as they eagerly examine famous masterpieces for detail and mood, even the Mona Lisa's smile can become less mysterious as, one by one, students gradually tire of this approach.

Daily vocabulary lists? Really? The same can be said for journal prompts. If I simply want students to write, then these spiral-bound classics fit the bill. But what if I want a bell-ringer to do more for my classroom than settle the class, one that can also enhance my curriculum instruction?

Could the bell-ringer format help support my standards-based lessons, foster collaborative learning, and also tap into critical thinking and creativity—as well as help me gain a few precious minutes to take care of classroom details?

Admittedly, this was an ambitious goal. But that was what I was looking for in a bell-ringer. I wanted even those first five minutes of class to engage students in the discovery of learning and to build their mental muscles—muscles that they could engage as they tackled higher-order skills or in my language arts lessons.

A Little Learning Theory

Respected learning theory supported the rationale behind my goal. As far back as 1938, John Dewey expressed dissatisfaction with the trend in education to ignore "the ability to think," which he felt was being "smothered... by an accumulation of miscellaneous ill-digested information." In 1962, educational psychologist and author Jerome Bruner wrote that the emphasis on discovery helped children learn the components of problem solving. In 1980, studies conducted by Dr. Joanne Hendrick, child development researcher, found that giving children a range of time to foster creative traits helps equip them with the tools necessary for being able to "think for themselves."

Going from theory to practice, however, has engaged even more discussion, as educators strive to determine the components of critical thinking. Most agree that all people possess potential areas of talents that can be developed through careful training and nurturing. The Talents Unlimited Model, under which I trained in post-graduate studies, focused on five main areas of development: communication, forecasting, decision-making, productive thinking, and planning.

This model, in turn, was based on the research of Calvin Taylor (1968) and his work on five-ability, or talent areas, not readily apparent through typical intelligence tests, and that of J.P. Guilford (1967). Guilford's interest in divergent and convergent thinking led him to believe that specific talents and abilities could be developed under the right conditions. Other educational researchers who have come to similar conclusions include L. L. Thurstone (1938), H. Gardner (1983), and R. J. Sternberg (1985).

Making Theory Come Alive in the Classroom

Today's data-driven classroom increasingly focuses on student performance on tests and, unfortunately, works against these research findings. While the development of critical thinking skills has become more commonplace in some settings (such as classes for gifted students), most language arts teachers at all levels find it difficult to include time for critical thinking into an already tightly scheduled day.

The time-limited bell ringer provides the perfect format to create time for regular and consistent practice with critical thinking skills while still addressing Common Core standards and providing support for the school's curriculum. In addition, Take Five! is naturally differentiated and engages reluctant learners with hands-on learning. It also fits well with regular or block-scheduled classrooms.

If critical thinking could become the focus for bell ringers, time management would perfectly integrate with standards to create an easy and engaging solution that is congruent with research and also extends its value beyond the first five minutes of class. That is the goal of Take Five!

But had I met that goal? The answer to that question came one day with an unexpected classroom visit from my assistant principal. By then, I was regularly harnessing the power of the critical-thinking bell ringer to engage minds and prepare students for the academic challenges of the 90-minute block.

That day, my ninth grade students were using their paperback copies of *The Giver* as a standard for a weight-bearing load in a bridge-building activity. There they were, tearing and tightly folding notebook paper and looping paperclips around string. The students murmured to each other–the white noise of critical thinking. No one looked up as the vice principal skeptically scanned the classroom.

"What's going on here?" he asked.

The students immediately answered: "We're thinking."

His eyes quickly darted to the board, searching to see what standards could possibly mesh with building a bridge in an English classroom.

Along with the regular standards, he saw the following: "Engage effectively in a range of collaborative discussions (one-on-one, in groups, and teacher-led) with diverse partners on topics, texts, and issues, building on others' ideas and expressing their own clearly." Indeed, that's exactly what they were doing.

When a student asked him to watch as she tested her team's creation, he gamely went over, observed, and even offered some advice, thus engaging in the collaborative discussion.

But the proof of the value of the approach became clear at the end of the year. When my state's assessment test scores came back, my principal shook his head in wonder. "Eighty-six percent learning gains. That's awesome!"

The next year, that pushed upward to 89 percent.

I share these figures, not to pat myself on the back, but to justify the use of critical-thinking bell ringers for language arts. For here's what I learned, and what I hope you will, too: when students are given the opportunity to tackle a challenge, to search and probe for a solution to an entertaining problem—no matter how trivial the problem may seem—that brief amount of invested time in mental activity transfers into wider applications in the subject area as well.

Chapter 1:
Getting Started

One of the prompts in this collection, "To Be or Not To Be" asks students to define a word in terms of what it **is not,** instead of what it **is**. This simple critical-thinking activity pushes students to categorize, to eliminate, to compare and contrast, to refine, and to reflect.

Let's apply the same principle to the word "prompt." A prompt is . . .

NOT

merely a means to give you time to take roll at the beginning of class.

a random busy-work assignment.

an isolated activity that is disconnected from classroom objectives.

a tool used to get a right or wrong answer.

Most importantly, prompts are not "fluff" activities, and although many are indeed fun, who says learning can't be?

This book includes a prompt for every day of the school year. Use them as you like. Choose among them to support your daily lessons, take them in order, repeat your favorites—it's up to you and your students.

The idea is simple. The posted prompt greets students as they arrive in class. Depending on the technology you have on hand in your classroom, you can access the prompts from the book or the CD. They are adaptable for everything from a traditional chalk board to an ELMO or interactive white board. You can even designate a student to read the prompt aloud for the class.

Some activities will require specific materials that are listed on the page with each prompt. Teachers will need to have these assembled and ready for the students as soon as they walk into the room. These can be placed in a basket for the students to retrieve. If time allows, individual supplies can be placed on each student's desk.

Some prompts will quickly become student favorites (Inventive Vocabulary, Name Game, and Looney Towns), and they will yield new responses each time the prompt presents itself through a few minor changes—variations that the students often like to make themselves.

Some prompts require written responses, while others may be hands-on encounters. For written responses, students can use a composition book or journal, a note card set (with spiral binding), or a folder on their computer, which I call the student's W.A.L.L. (Write a Language Link).

Much like its Facebook counterpart, the students' W.A.L.L. is the place where they will respond to a prompt. Here, they might problem-solve, write, describe, reflect, or plan.

Establishing the "Learning Setting"

A suggested Learning Setting for each prompt—individual, pair, or collaboration—appears in the Table of Contents and on each individual prompt page.

How you pair your students is up to you and your classroom. You can allow students to choose their own partners. Remember, though, that if left to their own devices, students generally will choose the same partners, so you might want to mix it up a little. You can, for example, allow students to develop their own partnering system.

You can also assign partners in several different ways, for example, partnering students at two different academic levels. I usually find that the more advanced student models the thinking skills for her partner and provides an excellent scaffold.

On other days, I use a Partner Pail, a container filled with slips of paper marked with a letter of the alphabet, with two slips for each letter (After you reach twenty-six, just label the slips AA and so on). This same system works for collaborative groups, too–just create the same number of like letters as you have partners. Or, if you prefer truly random partnering without all the paper, you can use an online tool like Research Randomizer (www. randomizer. org). Should behavior become a problem, quickly and simply switch students from one group to another.

Breaking Down the Components of Each Prompt

COMMON CORE STANDARDS

LANGUAGE ARTS LINK
These correlate with the Common Core Standards, providing teachers with immediate focus for the prompt, e.g. tone, main idea, inference, haiku, cause/effect.

LEARNING SETTING
This is either pair, individual, or collaboration.

SUPPLY LIST
All necessary materials to complete each prompt.

TEACHING TIP
This is supplemental information specifically for the instructor, e.g. suggestions, extension lessons, ideas for incorporating digital tools.

In addition to the 182 prompts included in Take Five, 100-plus extension lessons are also provided through the Teacher Tips.

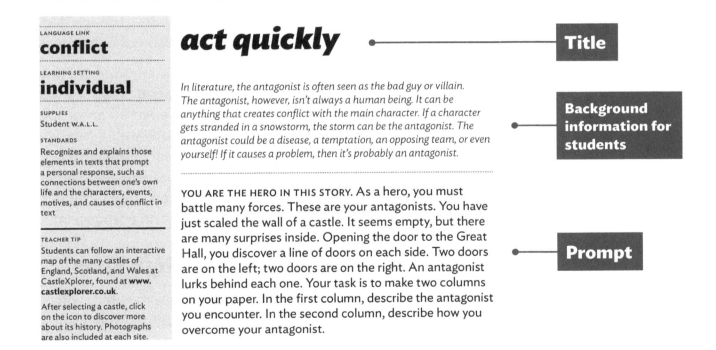

LANGUAGE LINK
conflict

LEARNING SETTING
individual

SUPPLIES
Student W.A.L.L.

STANDARDS
Recognizes and explains those elements in texts that prompt a personal response, such as connections between one's own life and the characters, events, motives, and causes of conflict in text

TEACHER TIP
Students can follow an interactive map of the many castles of England, Scotland, and Wales at CastleXplorer, found at **www.castlexplorer.co.uk**.

After selecting a castle, click on the icon to discover more about its history. Photographs are also included at each site.

act quickly ● — **Title**

In literature, the antagonist is often seen as the bad guy or villain. The antagonist, however, isn't always a human being. It can be anything that creates conflict with the main character. If a character gets stranded in a snowstorm, the storm can be the antagonist. The antagonist could be a disease, a temptation, an opposing team, or even yourself! If it causes a problem, then it's probably an antagonist. ● — **Background information for students**

YOU ARE THE HERO IN THIS STORY. As a hero, you must battle many forces. These are your antagonists. You have just scaled the wall of a castle. It seems empty, but there are many surprises inside. Opening the door to the Great Hall, you discover a line of doors on each side. Two doors are on the left; two doors are on the right. An antagonist lurks behind each one. Your task is to make two columns on your paper. In the first column, describe the antagonist you encounter. In the second column, describe how you overcome your antagonist. ● — **Prompt**

In addition to the 182 prompts included in *Take Five*, 100-plus extension lessons are also provided through the Teacher Tips.

Note that all of the activities support the two most important standards, which are not listed separately on each prompt. These standards are:

> Writes routinely over extended time frames for a range of tasks, purposes, and audiences

> Communicates in spoken, written, and visual form, for a variety of purposes and a variety of audiences.

Sharing Responses: "Pick Me, Pick Me!"

Sharing responses is an important learning opportunity that can be done at any time during class. If a language arts skill is first on the lesson plan agenda, then the prompt provides the ideal link to the lesson. If work is to begin on writing a summary, then pull up the prompt "Title Terror" and let the fun begin. A cross-index of Language Arts links is provided in the Appendix, listing language skills covered by each Take Five prompt.

On a typical day, I usually allow three or four responses to lead the way into that day's lesson. Since there is a prompt each day, all students will receive the opportunity to share, though I do occasionally call on the quieter students to make sure that happens.

On some days, the end of class may be a more appropriate time for student responses—for example, a collaborative response that required problem-solving tasks, such as "Mobile Art I" on p. 100. These collaborative prompts and responses work well when you have a little more time. I usually schedule these for days when I know the students will be more restless than usual—the day before a holiday, for instance. Surprisingly, even on these days, students follow the prompts with imagination, reflection, and enthusiasm.

Differentiating Instruction: "High Five!"

Some prompts in the *Take Five* collection are labeled with a High Five[5] sign, which is a superscripted number five. These markers alert teachers to prompts that may need some degree of background knowledge or a higher level of critical thinking. Bar graphs, for instance, might be an easy concept for one class, but more challenging for another group. For that reason, "Graph It I" (p. 68) would be designated with a High Five[5]. You, of course, will know which prompts fit the High Five[5] designation for your class.

Assessing Take Five! *Prompts*

Take Five! prompts can be assessed formally or informally. They can also be used to give feedback on how well students engage with the process of problem solving or be added to student portfolios as a record of practice for various critical-thinking skills.

Finally, they can be viewed simply as a way to settle the class and exercise their mental muscles before the day's lessons begin.

As for my own system, I do a little bit of everything. On the days when I am free to walk around the room and discuss the prompt with the students, a quick check of the Student W.A.L.L. serves as instant feedback. Occasionally, I may ask students to select one of their favorite responses for a particular type of writing and develop it into a draft for an essay that we will then take through the writing process, thus moving from formative (informal) to summative (formal) assessment What teachers do not want, however, is a menacing stack of journals staring them in the face, waiting to be graded.

Here are four assessment options to consider: Student Participation Monitor, Link To Language Writing Process Rubric, Student W.A.L.L. Assessment, and the Student Self-Assessment. The templates can be used as a part of the student's overall portfolio or individually as a measure of formative or summative assessment.

Whenever an assessment is used that will impact a student's grade, then the assessment/rubric should be provided to students ahead of time. There should be no surprises. Students need to know, for example, that the W.A.L.L. should show characteristics of logic, creativity, and reflection. The same holds true for other assessments. Copies of each could be placed in each student's computer folder, stapled to the first page of their spiral notebooks, or placed in their regular binder.

Student Participation Monitor. Use this chart (p. 7) periodically to observe students and their level of participation in the Take Five! prompts. Though student interest will vary from one activity to another, direct observation alerts teachers to levels of interaction, engagement, participation, and strengths.

Link to Language Writing Process Rubric. This rubric (p. 8) provides opportunities for extending writing assignments beyond the five-minute prompt. The prompt then functions as a brainstorming

Often, a quick stamp on the page serves just as well. You'll find that students don't want to miss getting their papers stamped.

activity. Students could later select the narrative prompts they would like to develop into a complete story. The rubric helps guide students through the writing process. The numeric grades provided are a suggestion only to show how a summative grade could be given.

Student w.A.L.L. Assessment. This rubric (p. 9) provides a grading tool for assessment. The Student w.A.L.L. maintains the student's written responses for *Take Five!* prompts. The w.A.L.L. can be a journal, notebook, note card flip book, or a folder on the student's computer. Responses may be in the form of narratives, expository writings, plans for a group activity, drawings, brainstorming, or graphs. For ease of assessment, make sure students date each entry.

"Take Five!" Student Self-Assessment. This valuable formative assessment tool (p. 10) allows students time to reflect on their responses and level of participation. This information can help guide future instruction by alerting teachers to key factors that elicit the best level of engagement and performance from each student: interests, learning setting, acknowledged areas of difficulty. To be an effective tool, however, this assessment should be given periodically, e.g., monthly or at the end of a grading period.

Student Participation Monitor

Student	Date	Date	Date	Date	Date
	4 3 2 1	4 3 2 1	4 3 2 1	4 3 2 1	4 3 2 1
	4 3 2 1	4 3 2 1	4 3 2 1	4 3 2 1	4 3 2 1
	4 3 2 1	4 3 2 1	4 3 2 1	4 3 2 1	4 3 2 1
	4 3 2 1	4 3 2 1	4 3 2 1	4 3 2 1	4 3 2 1
	4 3 2 1	4 3 2 1	4 3 2 1	4 3 2 1	4 3 2 1
	4 3 2 1	4 3 2 1	4 3 2 1	4 3 2 1	4 3 2 1
	4 3 2 1	4 3 2 1	4 3 2 1	4 3 2 1	4 3 2 1
	4 3 2 1	4 3 2 1	4 3 2 1	4 3 2 1	4 3 2 1
	4 3 2 1	4 3 2 1	4 3 2 1	4 3 2 1	4 3 2 1
	4 3 2 1	4 3 2 1	4 3 2 1	4 3 2 1	4 3 2 1
	4 3 2 1	4 3 2 1	4 3 2 1	4 3 2 1	4 3 2 1
	4 3 2 1	4 3 2 1	4 3 2 1	4 3 2 1	4 3 2 1
	4 3 2 1	4 3 2 1	4 3 2 1	4 3 2 1	4 3 2 1
	4 3 2 1	4 3 2 1	4 3 2 1	4 3 2 1	4 3 2 1
	4 3 2 1	4 3 2 1	4 3 2 1	4 3 2 1	4 3 2 1
	4 3 2 1	4 3 2 1	4 3 2 1	4 3 2 1	4 3 2 1
	4 3 2 1	4 3 2 1	4 3 2 1	4 3 2 1	4 3 2 1
	4 3 2 1	4 3 2 1	4 3 2 1	4 3 2 1	4 3 2 1
	4 3 2 1	4 3 2 1	4 3 2 1	4 3 2 1	4 3 2 1
	4 3 2 1	4 3 2 1	4 3 2 1	4 3 2 1	4 3 2 1
	4 3 2 1	4 3 2 1	4 3 2 1	4 3 2 1	4 3 2 1

HIGHLY ENGAGED	MODERATELY ENGAGED	SOMEWHAT ENGAGED	LITTLE PARTICIPATION
4	3	2	1

Link to Language Writing Process Rubric

Name			
Circle the type of writing:	persuasive	descriptive	personal
	narrative	expository	comparison/contrast

| ← High | 4 | 3 | 2 | 1 | Low → |

DRAFT	Draft shows full development of topic based on the prewriting	4
	Draft shows adequate development of topic based on prewriting	3
	Draft shows limited development of topic based on prewriting	2
	Draft shows little or no development of the topic	1
REVISION	Revision reflects meaningful changes in the essay	4
	Revision reflects adequate changes in the essay	3
	Revision reflects little development from previous draft	2
	Revision remains much the same as original draft	1
ESSAY	**Introduction**	
	Effectively engages the reader with insightful introduction and thesis	4
	Provides adequate introduction and thesis statement	3
	Shows limited development of introduction and thesis	2
	Little evidence of introduction or thesis	1
	Support	
	Effectively develops the thesis with specific supporting details	4
	Adequately develops the thesis with supporting details	3
	Limited use of supporting details	2
	Little development of the thesis; few supporting details	1
	Organization	
	Clear evidence of logically-arranged ideas; proficient transitions	4
	Adequate arrangement of supporting details; basic use of transitions	3
	Limited organization of ideas with few transitional words and phrases	2
	Lack of coherence; insufficient transitions	1
	Conclusion	
	Effectively captures main point of the essay; insightful reflections	4
	Adequately reinforces the key point of the essay; some reflection	3
	Basically recaps the details and repeats the thesis	2
	Little if any closure to the essay	1
	Language/Mechanics	
	Elevated word choice; complexity of sentence patterns; few errors	4
	Appropriate word choice and sentence structure; some errors	3
	Consistent problems with sentence patterns, usage, or spelling	2
	Numerous errors in language usage and mechanics	1

28–25	24–22	21–20	19–17
A	B	C	D

Student W.A.L.L.* Assessment

4	3	2	1
Strong evidence of higher-order thinking.	Some evidence of higher-order thinking.	Little evidence of higher-order thinking.	No evidence of higher-order thinking.
Entries reflect the writer's logic, creativity, and reflection.	Entries reflect some indicators of the writer's logic, creativity, and reflection.	Entries have significant lapses in logic, creativity, and reflection.	Entries display fragmented attempts at responding to each challenge.
Insightful connections to a variety of tasks.	Adequate connections to a variety of tasks.	Some attempt to connect to a variety of tasks.	Little or no commitment to tasks.

Assessing the Student W.A.L.L.

The Student W.A.L.L. maintains the student's written responses for Take Five! prompts. The Student W.A.L.L. may be in the form of a journal, notebook, note card flip book, or a folder on the student's computer. Responses may be in the form of narratives, expository writings, plans for a group activity, drawings, brainstorming, or graphs. Teachers who choose to assess the Student W.A.L.L. will find it beneficial for students to date each entry before responding.

*W.A.L.L. = **W**rite **A** **L**anguage **L**ink

Take Five! Student Self-Assessment

Name

1. On a scale from 4 to 1, how do you feel you addressed the prompts? (Check one)

    4 ☐   3 ☐   2 ☐   1 ☐

    4 = My best!   2 = I could have done much better

    3 = Overall, I think they were okay   1 = Not so good!

2. Which type of prompts did you enjoy the most? (Circle one)

    Individual   Pair   Collaborative

3. Describe a prompt that you particularly enjoyed. Explain why.

4. Describe a prompt that you felt was difficult for you. Explain why.

5. If you could repeat a prompt, which one would it be? Why?

6. Do you feel these prompts have helped you to think "outside the box"? Explain.

7. If you could write a prompt for *Take Five*, what would it be?

Part II:
Alphabetized Prompt Index

act quickly

In literature, the antagonist is often seen as the bad guy or villain. The antagonist, however, isn't always a human being. It can be anything that creates conflict with the main character. If a character gets stranded in a snowstorm, the storm can be the antagonist. The antagonist could be a disease, a temptation, an opposing team, or even yourself! If it causes a problem, then it's probably an antagonist.

YOU ARE THE HERO IN THIS STORY. As a hero, you must battle many forces. These are your antagonists. You have just scaled the wall of a castle. It seems empty, but there are many surprises inside. Opening the door to the Great Hall, you discover a line of doors on each side. Two doors are on the left; two doors are on the right. An antagonist lurks behind each one. Your task is to make two columns on your paper. In the first column, describe the antagonist you encounter. In the second column, describe how you overcome your antagonist.

EXAMPLE

Fire-breathing dragon   *Spray dragon with a fire extinguisher*

Four antagonists are ready to do battle–be quick!

Ready? Take Five!

LANGUAGE LINK
conflict

LEARNING SETTING
individual

SUPPLIES
Student W.A.L.L.

STANDARDS
Recognizes and explains those elements in texts that prompt a personal response, such as connections between one's own life and the characters, events, motives, and causes of conflict in text

TEACHER TIP
Students can follow an interactive map of the many castles of England, Scotland, and Wales at CastleXplorer, found at **www. castlexplorer.co.uk**.

After selecting a castle, click on the icon to discover more about its history. Photographs are also included at each site. As an extension, each student could select a different castle to research and then present findings in a PowerPoint presentation.

SUPPLIES

One sheet of plain paper

Markers, colored pencils, or crayons

Computer (opt.)

STANDARDS

Interpret words and phrases as they are used in a text, including determining technical, connotative, and figurative meanings, and analyze how specific word choices shape meaning or tone

TEACHER TIP

Students can set select an action figure and create their own comic at Super Action Comic Maker, found at **www. artisancam.org.uk/flashapps/ superactioncomicmaker**.

Here, they select the action figure, the background, and the dialogue to create their own comic book. When they are finished, they can print their final product.

action figures 1

Imagine a story about being lost in the desert. The characters are tired and thirsty as they stagger through the sandy landscape. Bright and cheerful details would seem out of place. That is why the tone created by the writer is so important!

When an author begins to write a story, many choices must be made aside from just the plot. One of the first considerations for legendary suspense writer Edgar Allan Poe was the creation of the tone: most often tragic, sad, or suspenseful. The tone is a writer's attitude toward the subject or the character developed through the author's words and details.

YOUR TASK IN THIS TAKE FIVE IS A TWO-PART CHALLENGE. First, you will select two "tone" words from the following list: angry, sad, humorous, fearful, bold, scared, happy, and desperate. Once the tone words are selected, fold the sheet of paper in half from top to bottom, then again from left to right. Reopen to reveal four squares.

In the top half, draw an alien, monster, or other action figure on the left side of the sheet so that it best reflects the first tone word selected. On the right side of the bottom half, draw the same figure again, but this time the figure should reflect the second tone word.* These two drawings will be used in tomorrow's task.

Ready? Take Five! 5!

If you are using a computer, use your paint or drawing tool to create the two action figures. Position them on a blank document by following the same directions given for the sheet of paper.

action figures 2

Once the tone is selected, the conflict is ready to be developed. Conflict takes place when there is a struggle between opposing forces. It provides the foundation of a story's plot. Both the conflict and the plot need to include details that best represent the tone.

RETRIEVE THE DRAWING FROM THE PREVIOUS DAY'S TAKE FIVE. Today, you will write two brief paragraphs about your action figure by placing it in a conflict or situation that best reflects the tone words selected. For example: Your figure is a strange-looking dog, and you have selected the two words "threatening" and "humor." You might write something like this on the top half besides the drawing: "Tammy and Anika are playing in the park when a stranger walks over to talk to them. Their dog, Lennie, senses danger. He sits on his hind legs with his paws raised like boxing gloves. A scowl is on his face."

On the bottom half, the story continues: "Suddenly, Lennie dashes away and grabs a water hose from a nearby lawn in his mouth. He then races around the stranger and pins him to the slide with the hose. As the stranger screams, Tammy keeps the water hose pointed in his direction, soaking him with water until help finally arrives while Lennie poses in a hero's stance."

The story quickly moves from threatening to humorous. The first picture shows Lennie in his threatening stance, and the second picture depicts Lennie in his winning pose. What conflict will your character encounter?

Ready? Take Five! 5!

LANGUAGE LINK
conflict

LEARNING SETTING
individual

SUPPLIES
Action Figure drawings

STANDARDS
Write narratives to develop real or imagined experiences or events using effective technique, well-chosen details, and well-structured event sequences

Interpret words and phrases as they are used in a text, including determining technical, connotative, and figurative meanings, and analyze how specific word choices shape meaning or tone

TEACHER TIP
Students can develop their mini comic strip by adding other details at a later time. They might even decide to continue their adventures! Students will enjoy having time to share stories with their classmates.

SUPPLIES
Student W.A.L.L.

STANDARDS
Demonstrate understanding of figurative language, word relationships, and nuances in word meanings

Develop the topic with relevant facts, definitions, concrete details, quotations, or other information and examples

TEACHER TIP
An extension of this prompt is to bring out markers and colored pencils so students can recreate the idiom in a visual cartoon.

More Common Animal Idioms:

Crying wolf
Eager beaver
Let the cat out of the bag
Playing possum
Raining cats and dogs
Road hog
Smell a rat
Stubborn as a mule
Horse sense
Badgering someone
The lion's share

animal antics

Just hold your horses! Even people who have never ridden a horse can do just that—stop whatever they are doing. Idioms pull together groups of words to create a new meaning. A doghouse may be the physical structure where the dog lives, but someone who is in the doghouse is someone who is in big trouble!

QUIT HORSING AROUND! DON'T HOG THE BLANKET! We're sitting ducks! When things aren't going well, animals get all the blame in the idiom game. Can you think of other examples of idioms that include the use of animals? For this challenge, create a list of four common idioms plus two original idioms. Use each original idiom in a sentence.

EXAMPLES

"He's frogged the competition!" (He's quicker than they are!)

"This skateboard is elephant proof." (So strong an elephant couldn't break it.)

Ready? Take Five! 5!

astro-logical 1

Whether describing a day at the beach or an exciting soccer game, writing that involves the senses allows the reader to see, taste, smell, hear, and even touch the supporting details. Descriptive writing creates a picture in the mind of the reader. Whether describing a person, a place, or a thing, the aim is to reveal a subject through vivid and carefully selected details. Descriptive writing does not tell; it shows.

AMAZINGLY, SCIENTISTS AT THE WALTERS PLANETARIUM have discovered a new star on the horizon. As the lead investigator on the team, you have the honor of naming the star.

What will it be called? What does it look like? What type of physical characteristics does it possess? On your note card, name this unique object and then describe it using vivid adjectives and active verbs.

EXAMPLE

Kyrial: An orange glow radiates from its rocky surface. Through the hazy outer layers of its thick atmosphere, tiny rays of light flicker from cliffs of towering quartz.

Be very specific in this descriptive writing challenge because tomorrow's Take Five activity will take the star from words to reality.

Ready? Take Five! **5!**

LANGUAGE LINK

descriptive writing

LEARNING SETTING

pair

SUPPLIES

Note cards

STANDARDS

Use precise words and phrases, relevant descriptive details, and sensory language to convey experiences and events

Demonstrate command of the conventions of standard English grammar and usage when writing or speaking

TEACHER TIP

A fascinating follow-up to this prompt is the 3-D Digital Universe video at Hayden Planetarium (**www. haydenplanetarium.org**).

The video maps all that is currently known about the universe. An extension to the Astro-Logical prompt would be for students to use their vivid imaginations to map or simply brainstorm the unknown, filling in the gaps found on the map with other constellations, planets, or galaxies.

problem solving

pair

SUPPLIES

Note cards

Markers or colored pencils

Computer paint or draw tools (opt.)

STANDARDS

Include multimedia components (e.g., graphics, images, music, sound) and visual displays in presentations to clarify information

Engage effectively in a range of collaborative discussions (one-on-one, in groups, and teacher-led) with diverse partners on topics, texts, and issues, building on others' ideas and expressing their own clearly

TEACHER TIP

This activity can also be transformed into an Astro-Logical III with a 3-D activity. Plain paper can be crushed, shaped, and then tightly wrapped with masking tape to secure shapes.

Odd extensions can be created in this same manner to add to the planet's shape. Use different colors of masking tape and markers for extra details. These can be added to the mobiles in the "Mobile Art" Take Five activity or secured along a coat hanger, stringing all the new planets together.

astro-logical 2

Research has recognized that critical thinking and problem-solving activities need to be included in daily instruction. In this task, the descriptive writing activity is taken one step further by creating a visual representation of the imagined star.

LET YESTERDAY'S DESCRIPTIVE WRITING ACTIVITY TAKE SHAPE today as you create a visual representation of this new planet. You will use paper and markers or a computer drawing tool to complete this task. Be sure to include special characteristics as described in the previous prompt.

Ready? Take Five!

babysitting basics

MARITZA, A NEIGHBOR WHO LIVES DOWN THE STREET, has developed the flu and needs to go to the clinic. Unfortunately, there is no one around to watch her active, seven-year-old son, Felipe.

Your mom has volunteered your services so that she can drive Maritza to the clinic. As soon as the door closes behind you, it dawns on you that the television is broken, and there aren't any toys lying around. Trying not to be nosy, you peek in the kitchen cabinets and find the following items: pots and pans, extra paper towels, a stack of paper cups, canned goods, and a box of graham crackers. Your problem worsens as thunder rumbles in the distance.

Your task is a tough one. How will you keep your young charge entertained for the next two hours indoors? Think of two different ways to use the items available (besides conking Felipe over the head) and place each idea in a graphic like the example shown. Next, place a star by your *best* idea.

....

Ready? Take Five! 5!

```
                entertainment
        ┌───────────────────────────┐
   Create a carnival              Play mummy by
   game by knocking               wrapping your
   down a paper cup               young charge in
   pyramid with a                 paper towels
   paper towel ball
```

LANGUAGE LINK

graphic organizer

LEARNING SETTING

individual

SUPPLIES
Student W.A.L.L.

STANDARDS
Introduce a topic clearly, previewing what is to follow; organize ideas, concepts, and information, using strategies such as definition, classification, comparison/contrast, and cause/effect; include formatting (e.g., headings), graphics (e.g., charts, tables), and multimedia when useful to aiding comprehension

TEACHER TIP
Another informational reading resource is the American Red Cross' Emergency Reference Guide, available on their Caregiving and Babysitting webpage (**www.redcross.org/babysitting**). Here, students will also find a Babysitter's Report Record along with other useful information.

cause-and-effect

individual

SUPPLIES

Student W.A.L.L.

STANDARDS

Introduce a topic clearly, previewing what is to follow; organize ideas, concepts, and information, using strategies such as definition, classification, comparison/contrast, and cause/effect; include formatting (e.g., headings), graphics (e.g., charts, tables), and multimedia when useful to aiding comprehension

TEACHER TIP

This prompt can be particularly effective if used in the last week in September during the American Library Association's annual Banned Books Week. Dozens of ideas and activities for extensions to this prompt can be found at the ALA's website: **www.ala.org/ala/ issuesadvocacy/banned/ bannedbooksweek/index.cfm**.

ban all books

If wind blows over the ocean, it creates waves. When children have no books at home, they often fall behind in reading. These two examples show how one thing can lead to another. This is called cause and effect. In the first situation, the wind (cause) produced the waves (effect). In the second example, the lack of books was the cause; falling behind in reading was the effect. A cause-and-effect strategy is used to show why things happen the way they do.

IN THE NOVEL *FAHRENHEIT 451* BY RAY BRADBURY, books are illegal. A person can be arrested just for owning a book. Some people even disappear, never to be seen again—all for their love (and possession) of a book. Just consider how different the world would be if all reading material (books, magazines, phone texts, song lyrics, instructions) were banned. On your W.A.L.L., list three potential effects.

Ready? Take Five!

be the whale

To compare two items is to show how they are alike; to contrast two items is to describe their differences. The purpose of a comparison/contrast is to learn more about the topic, no matter how different the two objects may be.

For example, how is a period like a stoplight? They are alike in that they both signal coming to a halt. Also, a period can be transformed, or changed, into another mark of punctuation, like the colon or semicolon. Similarly, the stoplight can change from red to green and then yellow.

Their differences go beyond the fact that a period is a mark of punctuation, and a stoplight is a traffic device. That would be the obvious answer. Instead, a difference could be that a period controls thoughts while a stoplight controls physical actions.

HUMANS AND ANIMALS AREN'T ENTIRELY DIFFERENT. Take dogs, for instance. Humans and dogs eat and sleep, move from one place to another, can sometimes sense danger, and enjoy a reward when they do something right.

But how similar is a whale? Forget about the obvious physical similarities between a whale and a person. True, they both have eyes, skin, mouths, and even fat.

For this challenge, you will need to plunge a little deeper to discover three similarities between you and a whale and three differences. Place your responses in a comparison/contrast chart.

Ready? Take Five! 5!

LANGUAGE LINK

comparison/contrast

LEARNING SETTING

individual

SUPPLIES
Student W.A.L.L.

STANDARDS
Use words, phrases, and clauses to create cohesion and clarify the relationships among claim(s), reasons, and evidence

Introduce a topic clearly, previewing what is to follow; organize ideas, concepts, and information, using strategies such as definition, classification, comparison/contrast, and cause/effect; include formatting (e.g., headings), graphics (e.g., charts, tables), and multimedia when useful to aiding comprehension

TEACHER TIP
Additional Take Fives could be used as extensions of this prompt by allowing students to make different comparisons:

humans and butterflies
humans and bears
mosquitoes and whales

LANGUAGE LINK

personal narrative

LEARNING SETTING

individual

SUPPLIES
Student W.A.L.L.

STANDARDS
Use precise words and phrases, relevant descriptive details, and sensory language to convey experiences and events

Use narrative techniques, such as dialogue, pacing, and description, to develop experiences, events, and/or characters

TEACHER TIP
An extension to this prompt will take students back in time as they listen to actual oral histories at the Smithsonian Institution Archives (**www.siarchives.si.edu/research/oralvidhistory_intro.html**).

Students can create their own collection of oral histories by interviewing people in the community. The Smithsonian Institute offers "The Smithsonian Folklife and Oral History Interviewing Guide" at **www.folklife.si.edu/resources/pdf/interviewingguide.pdf**.

biography benders

A personal narrative is a true story that has been written in the style of fiction. These stories deal with events that really happened. It has all the characteristics of a narrative—plot, characters, setting—yet it is based on the writer's real experiences.

AMERICA'S EARLIEST STORIES WERE PASSED DOWN from generation to generation by word of mouth. Oral traditions are still an important part of who we are today. Some stories might include an ancestor's first encounter with America; perhaps she traveled by ship from Ireland and stepped ashore to begin a new life in New York.

Suppose *you* were to write your own personal narrative—one, however, that completely reinvents who you are and how you have lived your life. Since this is your story, feel free to be as imaginative as possible!

EXAMPLE

"My family and I once lived in Paris, but, after I was falsely accused of spying, we emigrated, or moved, to Africa where we lived in a tent in the dry desert until . . ."

Get the picture? Write a very brief, yet inventive, personal narrative.

Ready? Take Five!

breakfast of champions

CHOCOLATE, MARSHMALLOW, WHOLE GRAIN, PUFFED RICE, naturally sweetened, fruit added—is there no end to the cereals that line grocery store shelves?

As the manager, you now have to make a crucial decision. Two popular brands will have to go, and you know that some of your regular customers won't be too happy about that.

As you carefully make your choices, consider your own personal philosophy: Do you feel the nutritional value of the cereal is an important consideration? Are you more interested in what will sell best, even if it is a sugary mouth of empty calories?

Be specific in your choices and then create a customer notice to attach to the areas where the two cereals will no longer be on display. Use your most apologetic tone to explain the necessary change.

Ready? Take Five! **5!**

LANGUAGE LINK

tone

LEARNING SETTING

individual

SUPPLIES
Student W.A.L.L.

STANDARDS
Demonstrate command of the conventions of standard English grammar and usage when writing or speaking

Produce clear and coherent writing in which the development, organization, and style are appropriate to task, purpose, and audience

Analyze the impact of a specific word choice on meaning and tone

TEACHER TIP
This Take Five can springboard to a quick extension exercise by taking a survey using the favorite brands of cereal enjoyed by students in the classroom. Following the survey, students can then depict the results in different types of graphs (e.g., pie chart, bar graph).

Students will also enjoy conducting a survey online by using one of the many survey tools such as SurveyMonkey found at **www.surveymonkey.com**. After all students have taken the survey, results are represented in a variety of charts and graphs.

problem solving

collaboration

SUPPLIES

Note cards

Paperclips

Popsicle sticks

Yarn

Masking tape

Sheets of paper

STANDARDS

Engage effectively in a range of collaborative discussions (one-on-one, in groups, and teacher-led) with diverse partners on topics, texts, and issues, building on others' ideas and expressing their own clearly

Develop the topic with well-chosen, relevant, and sufficient facts, extended definitions, concrete details, quotations, or other information and examples appropriate to the audience's knowledge of the topic

TEACHER TIP

Items used to construct bridges may vary. Use on a day when there will be time to test the structures, or the testing can be conducted during the next Take Five. This prompt can be repeated at a later date using different materials, even spaghetti noodles.

An excellent extension to this prompt is NOVA's "Build a Bridge," webpage where students use informational reading skills to correctly select the right bridge for the job. The site also includes a wealth of Teacher Resources: **www.pbs.org/wgbh/nova/bridge/build.html**

bridge builders

THE ANCIENT ROMANS WERE WELL KNOWN for their arched bridge design. Many of these bridges are still found in Europe, including the Pons Aemilius in Rome, Italy, built in 179 BC.

Today, your team will become bridge builders. Your challenge is to use the items provided to each team to create a bridge that will span a distance of twelve inches (a space created by two chairs or two tables separated).

Items may be used in any way (e.g., torn, rolled). The object is to see which team's structure will hold the most weight. Team members will slowly place one paperback book at a time upon their structure. The structure must hold for at least ten seconds after each additional book is stacked. Use all items or only a few.

Take Five to build your structure, and then set aside. When time is available, test each structure.

Ready? Take Five!

burial customs

Tree diagrams are graphic organizers that visually represent relationships between ideas. The trunk represents the main topic, and the branches group relevant facts or ideas.

IN ANCIENT EGYPT, PHARAOHS, THEIR FAMILY MEMBERS, and other high officials were buried with special items to use in the afterlife: food, oils, gold, chariots, etc.

Imagine that you are a pharaoh who is deciding what to include in your tomb. Create a Tree Diagram to list three unusual items you would want to have in your tomb and explain each choice.

Ready? Take Five! 5!

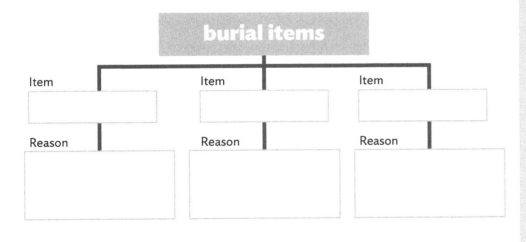

LANGUAGE LINK

graphic organizer

LEARNING SETTING

individual

SUPPLIES
Student W.A.L.L.

STANDARDS
Introduce a topic, organize ideas, concepts, and information, using strategies such as definition, classification, comparison/contrast, and cause/effect; include formatting (e.g., headings), graphics (e.g., charts, tables), and multimedia when useful to aiding comprehension

Introduce claim(s) and organize the reasons and evidence clearly

TEACHER TIP
Students can enter the world of Ancient Egypt at The British Museum's "Ancient Egypt" website: **www.ancientegypt .co.uk**. Interactive displays allow students to explore ancient burial customs.

persuasive writing

individual⁵

SUPPLIES

Bag of small items (e.g., leaf, coin, button, shell), enough for each student to use one

STANDARDS

Write arguments to support claims with clear reasons and relevant evidence

Use precise language and domain-specific vocabulary to inform about or explain the topic

TEACHER TIP

An extension for this activity allows students to test the credibility of their claims by holding an auction as students bid on the objects with the most desirable, or unusual, characteristics.

Another extension takes students behind the cameras as they produce and edit their commercial with video software such as Windows Live Movie Maker and Apple's iMovie.

buyer beware

At almost any moment, someone is trying to persuade you to buy a product or donate to a cause. Whether it is a public service announcement for "Toys for Tots" or a full-page advertisement for a certain car, these appeals all have one thing in common: they want their audience to do or believe something.

JUST HOW PERSUASIVE CAN YOU BE? Persuasive enough to convince someone to purchase a common rock? How about a twig, a coin, or a button?

From the bag, each person will select one item. Now it's time to get busy! Your task is to develop a script for a thirty-second commercial trying to sell this seemingly useless item.

You will need to stretch your imagination to make the ordinary extraordinary. What famous star might have popped that button; what military commander might have stepped on that twig? Carefully consider the kinds of appeals you might make to spur interest in your product.

Are there any bonus items if you order in the next thirty seconds? Let your imagination take your simple object to new heights.

Ready? Take Five! 5!

the case of the missing cockatiel

Writers are crafty people. Often they don't tell you all the details. Instead, they want readers to "read between the lines" to discover a deeper meaning. This is called making an inference. The clues are there; the reader just has to put them together.

NANCY DREW, THE TEENAGE DETECTIVE, HAS ANOTHER CASE on her hands and needs your team's help. This time, it's a race against the clock. She must solve this case in five minutes, or a thief will go free.

The crime: A very rare and expensive cockatiel was stolen from McTyre's Pet Shop. The only thing that appears the least bit out of the ordinary are a few grains of sand found just inside the back door of the shop. Witness Mark Snell, a late-night jogger, says he saw a dark van in the area at about eleven o'clock at night.

James Calloway, a local taxi driver, remembers seeing a light flick on and off in the shop around 9:30. Dean Sowell, shop owner, locked up at 9 p.m. but returned an hour later to retrieve his cell phone, which he had forgotten. He saw nothing unusual at that time.

Hmm . . . is there something fishy about their stories? You and your team must help Nancy solve this case. Revisit the testimony and evidence, then name the criminal and explain your decision. How did the clues lead you to this decision? How was the crook able to steal the bird? Use your imagination to break this case.

Ready? Take Five! 5!

SUPPLIES
Student W.A.L.L.

STANDARDS
Analyze how complex characters (e.g., those with multiple or conflicting motivations) develop over the course of a text, interact with other characters, and advance the plot or develop the theme

Cite strong and thorough textual evidence to support analysis of what the text say explicitly as well as inferences drawn from the text

Prepare for and participate effectively in a range of conversations and collaborations with diverse partners, building on others' ideas and expressing their own clearly and persuasively

TEACHER TIP
For this prompt, no one answer exists. This prompt allows students to develop their own imaginative—though logical—solutions.

Students can tests their deductive thinking skills with solve-it-yourself mysteries found at MysteryNet's "Kids Mysteries" at **http://kids.mysterynet.com**.

SUPPLIES
Student W.A.L.L.

STANDARDS
Assess how point of view or purpose shapes the content and style of a text

Analyze how and why individuals, events, and ideas develop and interact over the course of a text

Support claim(s) with clear reasons and relevant evidence using credible sources and demonstrating an understanding of the topic or text

TEACHER TIP
Though answers in this time frame will be brief and imaginative, students could go beyond this prompt to read about celebrities and the roles they turned down (like Will Smith, who turned down the starring role in *The Matrix,* or John Travolta, who passed on the chance to play the part of Forrest Gump).

This informational reading activity can be followed by an additional extension where students match actors to a novel or short story the class has just completed, one that has not yet made it to film.

character interview

Characterization can either be direct or indirect. In direct characterization, the author tells what a character is like. Indirect characterization develops through a character's words, thoughts, actions, appearance, and the reactions of other characters.

AS A REPORTER FOR THE LITERARY PRESS, you are to interview a literary character from a book or short story you have read.

First, decide who you will interview. Aside from his/her basic background information, there are three important questions you want to ask this character:

1. Why were you chosen for this role in the story?
2. What other character was considered for your part?
3. Why wasn't the other individual chosen?

Let your character answer these questions in his/her own words. Example: "Actually, I wasn't George Orwell's first choice for the role of Boxer, the horse, in *Animal Farm.* No, he had some crazy idea that Count Fleet would be better, but what kind of name is that for a horse who works on a farm? Besides, when Orwell was writing the story in 1945, Fleet was busy winning the Triple Crown— three of the biggest races in America—so he wasn't even available for the part. That's why he settled on me."

Now it's your turn.

Ready? Take Five!

cheat sheet

STUDENTS CAUGHT CHEATING IN SCHOOL are often punished, but students who use a cheat sheet while playing a video game are often rewarded with important game codes. These codes enable players to earn extra points and powers, change the appearance of a game, and even unlock special effects. However, you have to know the codes to make these things happen.

What would it be like if you were taking a test, and you had a cheat code of your own? Suppose by writing "addtostory," another paragraph were to magically appear. How helpful would that be when you are particularly short on words!

What if you just couldn't think of an ending for a plot you are creating for a narrative writing assignment? Write "endoftheend" and a conclusion suddenly materializes, drawing the action to a close. What are some other cheat codes that could help you when writing?

For this task, select four common writing problems you would like to master and provide a cheat code for each one. Just imagine—a cheat code for bonus points!

Ready? Take Five! **5!**

LANGUAGE LINK

writing process

LEARNING SETTING

individual⁵

SUPPLIES
Student W.A.L.L.

STANDARDS
Demonstrate command of the conventions of standard English grammar and usage when writing or speaking

Develop the topic with relevant facts, definitions, concrete details, quotations, or other information and examples

LANGUAGE LINK

characterization

LEARNING SETTING

individual

SUPPLIES
Student W.A.L.L.

STANDARDS
Analyze how and why individuals, events, and ideas develop and interact over the course of a text

Introduce a topic, organize ideas, concepts, and information, using strategies such as definition, classification, comparison/contrast, and cause/effect; include formatting (e.g., headings), graphics (e.g., charts, tables), and multimedia when useful to aiding comprehension

check it out 1

Much can be learned about people by looking at their bank accounts and the purchases they make. For instance, consider the following withdrawals: twenty dollars for a jazz CD; forty-five dollars at a seafood restaurant; forty dollars at the Humane Society; two hundred and fifty dollars for a set of ladies golf clubs.

From these purchases, you might infer that this person is a woman, probably older than thirty-five, who cares about animals, enjoys good food, is a music lover, and has the resources for hobbies and sports.

What about you? What would your purchases reveal about you if suddenly $300 were to appear in your bank account? How would you spend the money? You must make three very specific purchases, all closely related to the kind of person you consider yourself to be.

Create a three-column chart that lists the amount spent and the purchase in the first two columns. Use the third column to explain what these purchases reveal about you.

Ready? Take Five!

check it out 2

Now that you get the hang of the previous Take Five, try it again using a fictional character from a novel or short story you have recently read.

Ready? Take Five! 5!

LANGUAGE LINK

characterization

LEARNING SETTING

individual

SUPPLIES
Student W.A.L.L.

STANDARDS
Analyze how and why individuals, events, and ideas develop and interact over the course of a text

Introduce a topic, organize ideas, concepts, and information, using strategies such as definition, classification, comparison/contrast, and cause/effect; include formatting (e.g., headings), graphics (e.g., charts, tables), and multimedia when useful to aiding comprehension

LANGUAGE LINK

transitions

LEARNING SETTING

pair

SUPPLIES
Student W.A.L.L.

STANDARDS
Support claim(s) with clear reasons and relevant evidence using credible sources and demonstrating an understanding of the topic or text

Use a variety of transition words, phrases, and clauses to convey sequences and signal shifts from one time frame or setting to another

Introduce a topic, organize ideas, concepts, and information, using strategies such as definition, classification, comparison/ contrast, and cause/effect; include formatting (e.g., headings), graphics (e.g., charts, tables), and multimedia when useful to aiding comprehension

chocolate meltdown

Christopher Columbus just didn't get it! When he was offered cocoa beans, he thought, "Really? This is the best you've got?" Later, however, the explorer Cortez saw many possibilities in this Aztec wonder.

In fact, it was said that Emperor Montezuma was served up to fifty cups of this bitter liquid daily. Suppose, however, that chocolate did not make its way into the New World, but disappeared like the Aztecs.

Just think of what the world would be like without chocolate. Aside from not enjoying your favorite candy bar, think of four different effects it's absence would have on your day-to-day life.

Use the transitions below to complete each statement.

Are you ready to tackle this sweet task? Take Five!

The secret of chocolate disappeared when Emperor Montezuma died.	As a result,
	Thus,
	Therefore,
	Consequently,

choorubus

Descriptive writing uses sensory details and precise words to create images, moods, and emotions. It is writing that paints a picture for the reader through fresh, vibrant language.

Excitement has been building for weeks at the San Diego Zoo. The number of curious onlookers gathered outside the Choorubus cage has grown larger and larger with each passing day.

The object of all the attention is a nest where a female Choorubus, a nearly extinct species, has been patiently sitting, waiting the day when her newborn hatches.

Finally, the day arrives when the first cracks begin to appear, then more, until finally, finally . . . a loud gasp bursts from the crowd. The hatchling appears, but what emerges is beyond anyone's imagination. Your task is to describe and draw the newest Choorubus.

Ready? Take Five! **5!**

LEARNING SETTING

individual

SUPPLIES
Student W.A.L.L.

STANDARDS
Use precise words and phrases, relevant descriptive details, and sensory language to convey experiences and events

TEACHER TIP
Students can take a virtual tour of the San Diego Zoo on their website (**www.sandiegozoo.org**). Here, students can view live video of pandas, polar bears, elephants, and apes. The kid site offers a number of activities and games.

LANGUAGE LINK
figurative language

LEARNING SETTING
individual[5]

SUPPLIES
Student W.A.L.L.

STANDARDS
Analyze how a drama's or poem's form or structure (e.g., soliloquy, sonnet) contributes to its meaning

Use precise words and phrases, relevant descriptive details, and sensory language to convey experiences and events

Demonstrate understanding of figurative language, word relationship, and nuances in word meanings

TEACHER TIP
Students can later decorate their cinquains for display around the classroom.

A lively extension to this activity is to create a cinquain train where the teacher provides the cinquain and then the students use the last line to begin their own cinquains. For a more extended activity, the class can create a cinquain train on a classroom Kidblog account (**www.kidblog .org**) or another social network. When one student completes the cinquain, another picks it up from the last line.

cinquain design

"Silly cinquains, popular poetry, woven words." Can you hear the repetition of the initial consonant sound? This is called alliteration. This device occurs when the sound of one of those crazy consonants begins a word and is then repeated. It helps make a poem pop! Speaking of sound, anything that pops, bangs, screeches, rings, or buzzes uses another form of figurative language: onomatopoeia. This device creates words from sound.

SIMPLY STATED, A CINQUAIN IS A FIVE-LINE POEM. Aside from that, however, cinquains can go in many different directions. For this cinquain, you will be following these guidelines for each of the five lines:

Line One–one noun	*winter*
Line Two–two adjectives	*cold, icy*
Line Three–three nouns (alliterative)	*scarves, sleds, snow*
Line Four–four word phrase	*skating on frozen ponds*
Line Five–one word (onomatopoeia)	*splat!*

Select a noun for your topic that represents the current time of year, such as seasons, sports, celebrations, weather, etc.

Ready? Take Five! 5!

circular poetry

In a lyric poem, sensory details musically work together to convey an emotional experience.

ALONG THE SHORE, SEASHELLS GATHER until the tide takes them back to sea.

One such seashell is called the nautilus. This delicate creature began life in a tiny room that it built around itself. As it continued to grow, it built larger rooms that gradually wound their way around and around that first small room.

Early American poet Oliver Wendell Holmes wrote about this interesting sea creature in his poem, "The Chambered Nautilus." Eventually, the creature slips from the last chamber, and the empty shell is left behind. The poem infers that, as we grow, we also move forward, becoming a new person; we can't relive the past.

In today's challenge, create a short lyric poem that gives advice or offers a special insight into life. On your W.A.L.L., begin brainstorming the topic, rhyme scheme, and words you will be weaving together.

If you get stuck on the topic, think of another natural element (the trees in the fall, tiny grains of sand, eagles, earthworms, even mosquitoes). Finally, pull your ideas together to create a first draft.

Ready? Take Five! 5!

LANGUAGE LINK

poetry

LEARNING SETTING

individual[5]

SUPPLIES
Student W.A.L.L.

STANDARDS
Develop and strengthen writing as needed by planning, revising, editing, rewriting, or trying a new approach

Determine central ideas or themes of a text and analyze their development; summarize the key supporting details and ideas

TEACHER TIP
To better understand the focus of this challenge, a reading of Oliver Wendell Holmes' poem "The Chambered Nautilus" makes a fitting extension of this prompt.

A copy of this poem may be viewed at Bartleby.com (**www. bartleby.com/102/107.html**). More general information on nautilus shells can be obtained online at Sea and Sky: **www.seasky.org**.

SUPPLIES

Paper plate

Markers

STANDARDS

Use precise words and phrases, relevant descriptive details, and sensory language to convey experiences and events

Analyze how a drama's or poem's form or structure (e.g., soliloquy, sonnet) contributes to its meaning.

Include multimedia components (e.g., graphics, images, music, sound) and visual displays in presentations to clarify information

circular poetry 2

Today you will be finalizing the poem you began earlier and using the paper plate to publish your poem.

Start in the center of the plate, and then wind your words around the center until you reach the edge of the plate. Decorate with markers.

Ready? Take Five!

circus surprise

Description allows the reader to picture scenes, people, and events. Effective descriptive writing uses precise words and images.

After weeks of waiting, the circus finally pulled into town! Bailey was so excited. That afternoon, she and her sisters, Megan and Allie, rushed inside the big red tent and quickly took their seats in the stands.

Bailey couldn't wait to see the elephants; Allie's eyes were on the high-wire act as Megan searched for the clowns. Soon the stands were full. Vendors walked up and down the aisles selling popcorn boxes and tall cups brimming with peanuts.

At last, the ringmaster strode to the center of the ring. "Ladies and gentlemen! I know you are here to see the lions and elephants, the clowns and trapeze artists, fire-eaters, and dancing bears, but tonight we have an act that has never been seen on any continent, not in the entire world! It has action and thrills, danger, and beauty."

Megan looked at Bailey with eyes wide. "What can it be?" she whispered. Before Bailey could answer, a loud boom sounded; a rush of smoke filled the center ring, and then before their very eyes . . . .

What did they see? In this task, you must describe the circus surprise.

Ready? Take Five! 5!

LANGUAGE LINK

descriptive writing

LEARNING SETTING

individual

SUPPLIES
Student W.A.L.L.

STANDARDS
Analyze how an author's choices concerning how to structure a text, order events within it (e.g., parallel plots), and manipulate time (e.g., pacing, flashbacks) create such effects as mystery, tension, or surprise

Use precise words and phrases, relevant descriptive details, and sensory language to convey experiences and events

TEACHER TIP
Students will enjoy visiting the Ringling Bros. and Barnum & Bailey website at **www.ringling.com**. Their Fun Zone offers a number of fun activities.

LANGUAGE LINK

words and phrases

LEARNING SETTING

individual

SUPPLIES
Student W.A.L.L.

STANDARDS
Determine or clarify the meaning of unknown and multiple-meaning words and phrases by using context clues, analyzing meaningful word parts, and consulting general and specialized reference materials, as appropriate

Introduce a topic; organize ideas, concepts, and information, using strategies such as definition, classification, comparison/contrast, and cause/effect; include formatting (e.g., headings), graphics (e.g., charts, tables), and multimedia when useful to aiding comprehension

TEACHER TIP
This prompt can be repeated by using different word parts:

Suffixes:
Ize – to make
ly – to show how

Prefixes:
micro – small
in – not

Root:
aqu – water
astro – star

For a complete list of word parts see the Guide to Grammar and Writing website: **www.grammar
.ccc.commnet.edu**.

Students who would like to test their skills in *Jeopardy!* prefixes can go to: **http://grammar.ccc
.commnet.edu/grammar**

classroom jeopardy

Root words come from near and far; many are Anglo-Saxon, Greek, and Roman in origin. Word parts that precede a root word are known as prefixes while those that follow are called suffixes.

The root word "port" means to carry. Add the prefix "trans" and the word becomes transport," meaning to carry across. To describe something that can be transported, tack on the suffix "able" and it becomes transportable. Knowing the meaning of prefixes, suffixes, and root words can lead to an understanding of many new words.

"GREEN ANIMALS," "ARTFUL," "SO 'B' IT"—these phrases could easily be *Jeopardy!* categories by adding the key phrase "What is?"

"What is a frog?" (green animals);
"What is the 'Mona Lisa'?" (works of art)
"What is a honeybee?" (things that contain the "B" sound)

Unlike *Jeopardy!*, contestants in this game will list as many words as possible within the five-minute time period. These words will go into three categories.

First, make three columns on your paper. At the top of each column, write the following: TELE, RE, MENT.

The first category: words that contain the root word "TELE". The second category: words that contain the prefix "RE". The third category: words that contain the suffix "MENT".

What about telescope, rewrite, and development? Place your responses in the three columns.

Ready? Take Five! 5!

classy classics 1

"WHY DO WE ALWAYS HAVE TO READ CLASSICS?" Drena moaned to her teacher.

What exactly is classic literature, anyway? With a partner, develop a definition for the phrase "classic literature."

Write this definition on the paper provided and post it to a class wall, creating a collage of definitions.

Ready? Take Five!

LANGUAGE LINK

definition

LEARNING SETTING

pair

SUPPLIES

Strips of construction paper

Markers

STANDARDS

Engage effectively in a range of collaborative discussions (one-on-one, in groups, and teacher-led) with diverse partners, building on others' ideas, and expressing their own clearly

Develop the topic with relevant facts, definitions, concrete details, quotations, or other information and examples

TEACHER TIP

To set the stage for this prompt, an assortment of novels considered classics could be displayed in the classroom. The American Library Association maintains a Young Adult site that lists Best Books for Young Adults: **www.ala.org/yalsa/ booklists/bbya**. In addition, Minnesota's Hennepin County Library maintains an excellent and diverse list of teen reads at **www.hclib.org/teens/read.cfm**.

persuasive writing

individual

SUPPLIES
Student W.A.L.L.

STANDARDS
Compare and contrast texts in different forms of genres (e.g., stories and poems; historical novels and fantasy stories) in terms of their approaches to similar themes and topics

Write arguments to support claims with clear reasons and relevant evidence

classy classics 2

THE PREVIOUS CHALLENGE DEVELOPED WORKING DEFINITIONS for the phrase "classic literature." Today, you will consider books you have read that haven't met classic standards— until now.

What book do you think should now be considered a classic? Using the collage of definitions, write a persuasive argument for your choice. Be sure to refer to the definitions in the argument.

Ready? Take Five!

clay creatures 1

HEROES COME IN ALL SHAPES AND SIZES. There's Thor, Shrek the ogre, the Teenage Mutant Ninja Turtles, the Hulk, the X-Men, and the Transformers.

As a character designer, you and your partner will be creating an entirely new hero. Before the hero makes it to film, however, a prototype, or model, must first be made.

Using modeling clay, create an entirely different type of heroic creature. Let your creative side take charge of this challenge. When time is up, set the creature aside and mark it with your name for next time.

Ready? Take Five! 5!

LANGUAGE LINK

characterization

LEARNING SETTING

pair

SUPPLIES

Modeling clay

Paper plates

STANDARDS

Develop the topic with relevant facts, definitions, concrete details, quotations, or other information and examples

Integrate multimedia and visual displays into presentations to clarify information, strengthen claims and evidence, and add interest

TEACHER TIP

Claymation, animated video using clay creatures, takes this prompt to another fun level. Instructions for creating this mini-movie can be found at numerous sites on the Internet.

Start with this SlideShare presentation entitled "Claymation Instructions for Classroom": **www.slideshare.net/shines/ claymationinstructions-for-the -classroom**.

LANGUAGE LINK

characterization

LEARNING SETTING

pair

SUPPLIES

Note cards

Paper plates

STANDARDS

Develop the topic with relevant facts, definitions, concrete details, quotations, or other information and examples

Use narrative techniques, such as dialogue, pacing, and description, to develop experiences, events, and/or characters

clay creatures 2

It's time to put some life into your hero. Study the prototype carefully. What will be the specific qualities of this powerful figure? What is his or her history? On the note card, write a brief description and display the card with your hero.

Ready? Take Five!

coat of arms

In medieval times, knights dressed in their full armor could not be recognized. Who knew if they were friend or foe? To solve this problem, knights soon had their own coat of arms.

Usually, this was a shield that bore their emblem—typically a significant animal or symbol. Some knights might select a lion for its physical strength or a cross for its spiritual strength. A shield might also include the knight's motto, a saying that represents his family or code of conduct.

JUST AS KNIGHTS OF OLD HAD MOTTOS such as "peace and plenty," today many towns, businesses, sports teams, and organizations have their own mottos as well.

For example, the United States Marine Corps selected "Semper Fidelis," always faithful. For many years, Google's informal motto was "Don't be evil." One school selected "Have courage to be wise" to reflect their image, while another school chose, "Do well in all that you do."

In this challenge, you will create a personal motto, your code of conduct. On the strip of paper, write your motto. Add color and display.

Ready? Take Five!

LANGUAGE LINK

reflective writing

LEARNING SETTING

individual

SUPPLIES

Strips of paper

Markers

Desktop publishing software (opt.)

STANDARDS

Develop the topic with relevant facts, definitions, concrete details, quotations, or other information and examples

TEACHER TIP

This activity could be expanded by allowing students to create their own coat of arms.

For more information on coats of arms, visit the Fleur-de-lis Designs website: **www.fleurdelis.com**.

Students will also enjoy creating an interactive coat of arms that they can print after completing a series of design choices. Simply go to the Show Me website at **www.show.me.uk/topicpage/Art-and-Design.html** and click on the "Design a Coat of Arms" icon.

LANGUAGE LINK

parts of speech

LEARNING SETTING

collaboration

SUPPLIES

Red and white construction paper strips

Glue/staples

Markers

STANDARDS

Use a variety of transition words, phrases, and clauses to convey sequence and signal shifts from one time frame or setting to another

Demonstrate command of the conventions of standard English grammar and usage when writing or speaking

Follow rules for collegial discussions, set specific goals and deadlines, and define individual roles as needed

conjunction chain

Conjunctions serve as a bridge to join words, phrases, or clauses of equal importance. The coordinate conjunctions are as follows: for, and, nor, but, or, yet so. Gage and Cody play the guitar. Ellie likes Facebook, but Jen prefers Myspace.

A FAMILIAR DECORATION FOR PARTIES uses thin strips of construction paper glued end to end to create circles. Another circle (or link) is then made through the first circle, until finally a chain begins to emerge.

Today's task is to create a Conjunction Chain to create one very long sentence using white and red paper strips—a chain that keeps growing with the use of coordinate conjunctions, the red strips. Each white strip will contain one word, short phrase, or clause.

Each time a conjunction can be used, slip on a red strip with the conjunction written boldly in black. Remember to place a comma before a conjunction when it joins two sentences.

EXAMPLE

*Hunter **and** Tran ran onto the field, **but** their amazed teammates **and** the cheerleaders stared with eyes wide, **for** a deer **and** her fawn were following right behind them.*

Which team can make the longest chain in the time given?

Ready? Take Five!

criminally yours 1

When news reporters are gathering information for a story, they begin by asking questions. They want to answer the five w's: who, what, when, where, and why. Their news stories are objective, stating the facts without emotional involvement or personal point of view.

EVERY GOOD NEWS STORY REPORTS THE FACTS. The story will tell a reader *who* was robbed, *where* and *when* the crime occurred, *what* was stolen, and sometimes even *why* it occurred. But what was the complete story?

Using a local or national newspaper such as *USA TODAY*, find one news story. Use scissors to cut out the story. Next, read the story carefully while highlighting key phrases that answer the five w's.

Staple the clipping to a plain sheet of paper, then set aside. The rest of the story will appear in the next activity.

Ready? Take Five!

LANGUAGE LINK

main idea/ point of view

LEARNING SETTING

individual

SUPPLIES
Local or national newspapers

Scissors

Highlighter

Paper

STANDARDS
Read closely to determine what the text says explicitly and to make logical inferences from it; cite specific textual evidence when writing or speaking to support conclusions drawn from the text

TEACHER TIP
Many newspapers can be accessed online. Students can then cut and paste the information requested into their prompts.

main idea/
point of view

individual

Student W.A.L.L.

Write narratives to develop real or imagined experiences or events using effective technique, well-chosen details, and well-structured event sequences

Assess how point of view or purpose shapes the content and style of a text

criminally yours 2

TODAY'S TAKE FIVE GOES FROM FACT TO FICTION. Retrieve the newspaper clipping, then, using your very vivid imagination, transform the information from a news story to a creative narrative, describing the events from the *criminal's* or *victim's* point of view.

Ready? Take Five!

death by chocolate

When writers want to recreate a sensory experience, they use imagery—descriptive words and phrases. It might be the deep wail of a ship's foghorn at night, a damp wind, the smell of freshly baked cookies, or the taste of rich dark chocolate.

When Valentine's Day arrives, chocolate is soon to follow. This February, many people will unwrap a sweet surprise and enjoy every creamy bite. Some will enjoy expensive chocolates while others bite down on the cheaper, more popular, brands. Is there really a difference in chocolates?

In your group, you will find three paper plates containing small samples of chocolate. The plates are labeled A, B, and C. On your paper, make three columns. Label the columns A, B, and C. Your task is to sample a piece of chocolate from each plate. Be sure to savor each piece.

Next, record in the appropriate column the adjectives and descriptive phrases that come to mind for each of the three samples of chocolate. Was it rich or bitter? Did it melt slowly or not at all? What about the sweetness level?

Try to include at least three entries per column and star your favorite. A thesaurus is allowed. Share your findings before the actual identities of the chocolates are revealed.

Ready? Take Five!

LANGUAGE LINK

descriptive writing

LEARNING SETTING

collaboration

SUPPLIES

Student W.A.L.L.

Plastic containers with small pieces of chocolate: three well-marked containers per group. Choose chocolate ranging from decadent samples to cheaper brands that have no identifiable markings.

Small paper plates

STANDARDS

Use precise words and phrases, relevant descriptive details, and sensory language to convey experiences and events

Introduce a topic; organize ideas, concepts, and information, using strategies such as definition, classification, comparison/contrast, and cause/effect; include formatting (e.g., headings), graphics (e. g., charts and tables), and multimedia when useful to aiding comprehension

TEACHER TIP

Always check to make sure students and their allergies are taken into consideration.

For this activity to be reliable, chocolates need to be of the same type.

A fascinating 15-minute video entitled "Chocolate Production," about the making of chocolate can be viewed on YouTube: **www.youtube.com/watch?v=Tez9RZZIwC8**

SUPPLIES
Student W.A.L.L.

STANDARDS
Use words, phrases, and clauses to clarify the relationships among claim(s) and reasons

Develop the topic with relevant facts, definitions, concrete details, quotations, or other information and examples

TEACHER TIP
The Encyclopedia Mythica includes a webpage entitled the "Origin of the names of the days," which explains the real origins of the weekday names: **www.pantheon.org/miscellaneous/origin_days.html**.

eight days a week

MONDAY, TUESDAY, WEDNESDAY, THURSDAY, FRANZDAY, Friday . . . Franzday? What if there really was an extra day in the week?

The task today is to consider this new day of the week. Like the other weekdays, this one will also be named after a god, the fictitious Norse god Franzor.

Who was the god Franzor, and what special powers did he possess? How should people observe Franzday? What is its special significance?

Ready? Take Five!

emoticons

WHAT E-MAILS AND TEXTS LACK, EMOTICONS PROVIDE. One wacky face slipped into a conversation can tell the reader if the message was meant to be funny, sad, or sarcastic.

From those first happy and sad faces, the world of emoticons exploded. Now, almost any tone can be reinforced through a wide variety of emoticons.

In this task, however, the teacher isn't quite sure what tone the writer is trying to portray. Your help is needed. Create a variety of emoticons to be occasionally placed in an individual's writing to alert the reader to the tone.

In this task, pairs will work together to create an appropriate and unique emoticon for five of the following tone words: lazy, joyful, hurt, scheming, depressed, nervous, calm, proud, and disappointed.

Ready? Take Five!

LANGUAGE LINK

tone

LEARNING SETTING

pair

SUPPLIES
Student W.A.L.L.

STANDARDS
Determine the meaning of words and phrases as they are used in a text, including figurative and connotative meanings; analyze the impact of a specific word choice on meaning and tone

Introduce a topic clearly, previewing what is to follow; organize ideas, concepts, and information, using strategies such as definition, classification, comparison/contrast, and cause/effect; include formatting (e.g., headings), graphics (e.g., charts, tables), and multimedia when useful to aiding comprehension

figurative language

individual

SUPPLIES

Student W.A.L.L.

STANDARDS

Demonstrate understanding of figurative language, word relationships, and nuances in word meanings

Use precise words and phrases, relevant descriptive details, and sensory language to convey experiences and events

exaggerate

When writers stretch details in their writing, exaggerating physical appearances or events, they are using a literary element known as hyperbole.

"IF I'VE TOLD YOU ONCE, I'VE TOLD YOU A MILLION TIMES!" Falin exclaimed. Really? A million?

"They can hear your screaming all the way to Canada," Laura calmly replied. Sound can travel that far, huh?

"My backpack weighs a ton," Chase groaned. Two books, and you're looking at a ton?

Many students have become masters of exaggeration, particularly when chores are assigned—"This is backbreaking work," "I'll die if I have to clean my room!"

Many writers have successfully used exaggeration, or hyperbole, in their writing. Mark Twain used it to help create humor. In his novel *A Connecticut Yankee in King Arthur's Court*, he wrote: "There did not seem to be brains enough in the entire nursery, so to speak, to bait a fish-hook with."

Hyperbole will be the key in addressing this prompt. Use hyperbole to describe two of the following situations: tired after a long day at school, losing a game by one point, not getting invited to a birthday party, being grounded, being chosen for a special award, or being saved from disaster.

Ready? Take as long as you want. Whoops—I'm exaggerating! Take Five!

fad today, gone tomorrow

FADS COME AND FADS GO. Many years ago, dance contests would last through the night to see which couple would last the longest on the dance floor. In the 1950s, teenagers enjoyed dropping coins into the jukebox to hear the latest record play, wearing poodle skirts, and seeing how many students could squeeze into a telephone booth at one time!

During the sixties, fads took a new direction with tie-dyed shirts, love beads, peace signs, and Ouija boards to tell the future. While some fads tend to surface again, one current fad just has to go! What will that fad be?

On your paper, list several current fads and then select one that truly annoys you. Next, write a persuasive letter to your classmates, urging them to help make this fad disappear for good!

Ready? Take Five! 5!

LANGUAGE LINK

persuasive writing

LEARNING SETTING

individual

SUPPLIES
Student W.A.L.L.

STANDARDS
Introduce claim(s) and organize the reasons and evidence clearly

LANGUAGE LINK

dialogue

LEARNING SETTING

individual

SUPPLIES
Student W.A.L.L.

STANDARDS
Demonstrate command of the conventions of standard English capitalization and punctuation when writing or speaking

Analyze how particular lines of dialogue or incidents in a story or drama propel the action, reveal aspects of a character, or provoke a decision

---

TEACHER TIP
More Famous Last Words:

"Am I dying, or is this my birthday?"
–Nancy Astor

"How were the receipts today at Madison Square Garden?"
–P.T. Barnum

"Now comes the mystery."
–Henry Ward Beecher

"Friends, applaud. The comedy is finished."
–Ludwig van Beethoven

"I am not the least afraid to die."
–Charles Darwin

"I must go in. The fog is rising."
–Emily Dickinson

"Now I shall go to sleep. Goodnight."
–Lord Byron

More famous last words can be found on The Phrase Finder website: **www.phrases.org.uk/ quotes/last-words**.

famous last words

ACCORDING TO MANY ACCOUNTS, the following last words were spoken by these notable individuals: "Go away; I'm all right."—H.G. Wells, author of *The Time Machine* and *The War of the Worlds*; "Is it the fourth?"—Thomas Jefferson (he died on the Fourth of July); "Cool it, brothers."—Malcolm X, human rights activist.

What possibilities exist for the last moments of the Joker, the Big Bad Wolf, the Gingerbread Man, Humpty Dumpty, or Blackbeard the pirate? Use these or any other characters to develop their famous last words. These words should reflect their personalities, their career choices, or their notoriety.

Use a minimum of two characters. Don't forget to use correct punctuation for each quote.

Ready? Take Five!

field trip

To be effective, setting goes beyond mere time and a place; it evokes an experience, a mood that is stamped indelibly into that scene: a chilly New England morning at the turn of the century, a countryside overflowing with the fruits of the fall season.

Consider the setting of your favorite book. Just imagine a land where vampires, dragons, magical horses, fantastical monsters, or pirates roam.

Your task is to select such a destination for the next classroom fieldtrip. At the top of your paper, draw a small box and write the specific setting—any time, any place.

From the bottom of the box, draw a line from each end. Alongside the first line, make a list of four items we will need to take with us. Beside the second line, make a list of four possible dangers that the class might encounter.

Ready? Take Five! 5!

SETTING

SUPPLIES
Student W.A.L.L.

Computer paint/draw tool (opt.)

STANDARDS
Introduce a topic clearly; organize ideas, concepts, and information, using strategies such as definition, classification, comparison/contrast, and cause/effect; include formatting (e.g., headings), graphic (e.g., charts, tables), and multimedia when useful to aiding comprehension

Use precise words and phrases, telling details, and sensory language to convey a vivid picture of the experiences, events, setting, and/or characters

LANGUAGE LINK

sequencing

LEARNING SETTING

pair

SUPPLIES

Sheet of plain paper

Stamp pad

Pen

STANDARDS

Write narratives to develop real or imagined experiences or events using effective technique, well-chosen details, and well-structured event sequences

TEACHER TIP

For inspiration, sample comic strips could be on display, such as comics that depict a main point, a lesson learned, or food for thought.

After all of the comics have been created, bind them together in a booklet. Students can add a title page with their name in the byline. More pages and adventures could be added in a later Take Five session.

fingertip comics 1

MOVE INTO PAIRS FOR THIS COMICAL VENTURE. This task involves making fingertip characters and a script to complete the storyboard for your comic.

Begin the process by taking a sheet of paper and folding it in half lengthwise, then horizontally. This will divide the paper into four equal squares. Use a pen or marker to trace along the fold lines.

Next, write a brief script for a cartoon that will easily fit into these four boxes. It can be an action cartoon, or perhaps a cartoon that develops a main point.

The most important element in this challenge, however, is a clear sequence of events or ideas. The contents of each square must flow naturally to the next.

Ready? Take Five!

fingertip comics 2

IT'S TIME TO ILLUSTRATE THE SCRIPT created in yesterday's Take Five challenge. Using the stamp pad, create the characters for your comic by pressing a fingertip into the stamp pad and applying it to the first square. Repeat until the comic is complete.

To create the characters' bodies, use vertical and horizontal fingerprints. A pen can be used to add text and details.

Ready? Take Five!

SUPPLIES

Sheet of plain paper

Stamp pad

Pen

STANDARDS

Write narratives to develop real or imagined experiences or events using effective technique, well-chosen details, and well-structured event sequences

SUPPLIES

Sheets of construction paper

Markers

STANDARDS

Develop the topic with relevant facts, definitions, concrete details, quotations, or other information and examples

Introduce a topic clearly, previewing what is to follow; organize ideas, concepts, and information, using strategies such as definition, classification, comparison/contrast, and cause/effect; include formatting (e.g., headings), graphics (e.g., charts, tables), and multimedia when useful to aiding comprehension

TEACHER TIP

After completing this activity, cut out the hands and display together under a title such as "Helping Hands" or "Give us a Hand!"

fingertip personality

ACCORDING TO MANY FORTUNETELLERS, the palm of a person's hand can tell the future of an individual: love life, the number of children, even health.

But what about one's fingertips? On your paper, trace your hand. On each fingertip, write one personality trait you would like to develop in the coming years (being more patient, helpful, honest, etc.).

Ready? Take Five!

fish out of water

TODAY'S PROMPT IS LIKE A FISH OUT OF WATER, a kangaroo without a pouch, or even a zebra without its stripes.

Select any creature and compare it to something that seems to have no similarities at all. For instance, how is a fish like a rose? They both grow, have a tough exterior (scales and thorny stalks), give off an odor, need nourishment, can be seen on a dinner table, and have four letters in their names.

In today's task, you will select any animal and compare it to one of the following: a type of tree, a book, an airplane, a pot of soup, a baby, or a piece of fruit.

Brainstorm to think of the many different ways the two things are similar. Use a comparison/contrast chart to record your observations.

Ready? Take Five! **5!**

LANGUAGE LINK

comparison/ contrast

LEARNING SETTING

individual[5]

SUPPLIES
Student W.A.L.L.

STANDARDS
Introduce a topic clearly, previewing what is to follow; organize ideas, concepts, and information, using strategies such as definition, classification, comparison/contrast, and cause/effect; include formatting (e.g., headings), graphics (e.g., charts, tables), and multimedia when useful to aiding comprehension

Introduce a claim(s) and organize the reasons and evidence clearly

TEACHER TIP
More Take Five prompts can evolve from this one by having students contribute slips of paper with nouns of persons, places, or things written on them. Students then pull two slips from the bag and write their innovative comparisons.

LANGUAGE LINK
cause-and-effect

LEARNING SETTING
individual

SUPPLIES
Student W.A.L.L.

STANDARDS
Provide a conclusion that follows from and reflects on what is experienced, observed, or resolved over the course of the narrative

Analyze how and why individuals, events, and ideas develop and interact over the course of a text

foggy footsteps

When writing a story, an author knows his or her audience loves the unexpected— within reason. To be believable, actions must remain true to a character.

AN EARLY MORNING FOG COVERS THE PATH YOU TAKE each day to the bus stop. Familiar objects now appear as ghostly outlines on each side of the path. A slight chill prickles your skin as you hear footsteps approaching from behind.

Somewhat spooked, you pick up your pace only to find that the footsteps quicken their pace as well. The bus stop lies far ahead in the shadowy distance.

Do you break into a fast run, turn and confront the unknown individual, or do something else? Time is running out. Hurry!

On your W.A.L.L., explain the decision you make and the outcome of that decision.

Ready? Take Five!

follow the clues

You pass a fellow student yawning as she slowly climbs the steps to the school. In one hand, she has a stack of vocabulary words and definitions, and in the other, a power drink. There are dark circles beneath her eyes.

Based on the above information, what can you infer, or guess, about this student? That she has stayed up all night studying for a vocabulary test? You're right!

Here is another example: A student walks the hall wearing a football tee shirt. His face is painted like a tiger, and he is visibly excited. What could you infer about this student?

The inference game is an easy one. You simply provide three clues and let someone else make the correct inference.

On your paper, create one set of inference clues (at least three). Next, read the clues aloud to your teammates and see if they can make the correct connection.

Ready? Take Five! 5!

LANGUAGE LINK

inference

LEARNING SETTING

collaboration[5]

SUPPLIES
Student W.A.L.L.

STANDARDS
Cite several pieces of textual evidence to support analysis of what the text says explicitly as well as inferences drawn from the text

TEACHER TIP
Interactive inference games can be found on Gamequarium's "Readquarium" webpage: **www.gamequarium.com/ readquarium/skillsi-p.html.**

LANGUAGE LINK

persuasive writing

LEARNING SETTING

individual

SUPPLIES
Student W.A.L.L.

STANDARDS
Demonstrate command of the conventions of standard English capitalization, punctuation, and spelling when writing

Write arguments to support claims with clear reasons and relevant evidence

food for thought

Two of the most common appeals in persuasive writing are emotional and logical. Love, pride, and respect are typical emotional appeals. Logical appeals may use facts, statistics, and other forms of logic.

HOW MUCH DO YOU WEIGH? NOW, THAT'S A WEIGHTY TOPIC! Many restaurants are helping their customers make healthy eating choices by posting the calorie and fat content of each item on the menu.

But what about at home? Clara is getting worried about her little brother, Thomas. Since their parents work late nights, no one is around to keep him from snacking on chips and cookies. At just nine years old, he is already packing on the pounds.

Clara needs your help. Write a letter to Thomas with your best advice and your most persuasive appeals. Warning: He's pretty stubborn, so you will need to have three good reasons why he needs to cut the calories.

Ready? Take Five!

future history

ARCHAEOLOGISTS LOVE TO GO DIGGING IN THE DIRT. They never know what artifacts they might find as they sift through the earth.

They do know that they can learn a great deal of information from what they find. If archaeologists uncovered a small village, for example, the artifacts could reveal how advanced its inhabitants were. They could also learn about the kinds of food the villagers ate, their religious customs, their form of currency, their defenses, etc.

Imagine that you are an archaeologist 200 years from now going on a dig in your current neighborhood. Gradually, you make you way down to the current time period. What three items do you find, and what do these items say about your neighborhood's inhabitants?

Use this information to write your report for the National Museum of American History.

Ready? Take Five! **5!**

LANGUAGE LINK

expository writing

LEARNING SETTING

collaboration

SUPPLIES
Student W.A.L.L.

STANDARDS
Write informative/explanatory texts to examine a topic and convey ideas, concepts, and information through the selection, organization, and analysis of relevant content

Introduce claim(s) and organize the reasons and evidence clearly

---

TEACHER TIP
The Society for American Archaeology provides a comprehensive listing of interactive activities related to archaeology. These can be found at **www.saa.org/publicftp/ PUBLIC/links/websites_kids .html**.

LANGUAGE LINK

graphic organizers

LEARNING SETTING

individual⁵

SUPPLIES
Student W.A.L.L.

STANDARDS
Introduce a topic clearly, previewing what is to follow; organize ideas, concepts, and information, using strategies such as definition, classification, comparison/contrast, and cause/effect; include formatting (e.g., headings), graphics (e.g., charts, tables), and multimedia when useful to aiding comprehension

Use narrative techniques, such as dialogue, pacing and description, to develop experiences, events, and/or characters

ghostly visitors

SIMILAR TO SCROOGE'S EXPERIENCE IN CHARLES DICKENS' *A Christmas Carol*, three nighttime visitors will soon be knocking at your door.

Do not fear these nightly visitations, however. The Ghost of School Years Past will send you back to the most exciting school year you have yet to experience. What made it so memorable?

The Ghost of School Years Present will take you to the most significant event of the current year (seeing a new baby brother for the first time, for example). Describe this event.

Finally, with the Ghost of School Years Yet to Come, you will soar high overhead. Here you will see the college, vocational school, military service, or alternate opportunity that awaits you. Where does the ghost take you?

Make a three-column organizer like the one below and record your findings. Be sure to label each column.

Ready? Take Five!

Schools Past	Schools Present	Schools Future

going purple

People, places, and products all seem to be "going green," a phrase that means becoming more eco-friendly as we work together to improve the health of our planet.

As individuals, we can be more responsible by recycling, conserving energy, and avoiding products that contain toxic chemicals. Businesses, schools, and cities are also getting involved by investing in and promoting eco-friendly alternatives.

Now, however, a new trend is taking place: "Going Purple." What is the message behind "Going Purple," and what can people do to help support this cause?

Ready? Take Five! **5!**

LANGUAGE LINK

expository writing

LEARNING SETTING

individual

SUPPLIES
Student W.A.L.L.

STANDARDS
Introduce a claim(s) and organize the reasons and evidence clearly

Interpret information presented in diverse media and formats (e.g., visually, quantitatively, orally) and explain how it contributes to a topic, text, or issue under study

LANGUAGE LINK
graphic organizer

LEARNING SETTING
pair[5]

SUPPLIES
Student W.A.L.L.

STANDARDS
Introduce a topic clearly, previewing what is to follow; organize ideas, concepts, and information, using strategies such as definition, classification, comparison/contrast, and cause/effect; include formatting (e.g., headings), graphics (e.g., charts, tables), and multimedia when useful to aiding comprehension

Interpret information presented in diverse media and formats (e.g., visually, quantitatively, orally) and explain how it contributes to a topic, text, or issue under study

TEACHER TIP
Newspapers such as *USA Today* contain a variety of graphs. These can be clipped and displayed for today's Take Five.

Students just beginning to learn the concept of a bar graph will enjoy dragging creatures to a bar graph. The end result is a colorful graph. This game can be found on PBS Kids' "Cyberchase" webpage: **www.pbskids.org/cyberchase/games/bargraphs/bargraphs.html**.

graph it 1

GRAPHS FREQUENTLY APPEAR ALONGSIDE MAGAZINE or newspaper articles to illustrate the content visually. They allow the reader to quickly grasp information such as how prices today differ from those ten years ago.

Now it's your turn to create a graph. On your paper, draw a very large letter L. This is your graph. Next, list the numbers one through ten alongside the vertical line, starting with zero. Across the bottom of the L, the graph will need the labels "Mosley," "Arnold," and "Bay." These names represent the schools in one town.

The line on the left side will show how many football games each school has won this season. If Mosley won four, Arnold five, and Bay three, how would the bar graph for each appear?

First, plug in the data on the bar graph for the three schools. Next, compare your graph with your partner's to check your results.

Ready? Take Five!

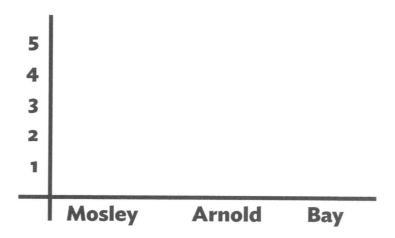

graph it 2

YESTERDAY'S TAKE FIVE INVOLVED the creation of bar graphs to visually represent the wins of three football teams. In today's challenge, you will be surveying your classmates to develop your own graph. First, consider what information you would like represent.

EXAMPLES

Favorite NFL teams

Classroom eye colors

Shoe sizes

Favorite ice cream flavors

Favorite colors

Ratio of boys to girls

Next, use your W.A.L.L. to record classmate responses. Make a tally mark when you receive a duplicate response. The following example shows a tally of birthday months.

Birthdays: August–HHII = 7   March-III= 3   May-II= 2

Once all responses have been tallied, create your bar graph. To continue with the above example, we would place a row of numbers (however many students were polled) along the left side of the chart. Along the bottom, we would list the months and then draw the bars to match our results.

While it may not be possible to survey everyone in the class in the time given, you will receive enough data to plug into a graph.

Ready? Take Five! 5!

LANGUAGE LINK

graphic organizer

LEARNING SETTING

individual⁵

SUPPLIES

Student W.A.L.L.

STANDARDS

Introduce a topic clearly, previewing what is to follow; organize ideas, concepts, and information, using strategies such as definition, classification, comparison/contrast, and cause/effect; include formatting (e.g., headings), graphics (e.g., charts, tables), and multimedia when useful to aiding comprehension

Interpret information presented in diverse media and formats (e.g., visually, quantitatively, orally) and explain how it contributes to a topic, text, or issue under study

TEACHER TIP

Students can input their information into the graph found at the National Center for Education Statistics Kids' Zone: **www.nces.ed.gov/nceskids/createagraph**.

SUPPLIES

Cardstock or construction paper

Used greeting cards

Glue

Computer paint/draw tools (opt.)

STANDARDS

Use precise words and phrases, relevant descriptive details, and sensory language to convey experiences and events

Include multimedia components (e.g., graphics, images, music, sound) and visual displays in presentations to clarify information

TEACHER TIP

A simple greeting card tool is available at Kerpoof Studio at **www.kerpoof.com**. Students make selections along the way and then print their creations.

greetings

A picture may paint a thousand words, but in this challenge, precise words and phrases will support the images torn from used greeting cards.

SOME OF THE MOST POPULAR GREETING CARDS TODAY are e-cards. These electronically delivered cards have simplified the way we send a birthday card or invitation; it's just a click away. Still, many people enjoy finding a greeting card tucked inside the mailbox, beside their breakfast plate, or in a backpack or lunchbox.

In today's challenge, you will become a greeting card writer. First, decide what your message will be: "Can't wait for summer to get here!"; "Hope your flu flies!"; "Our team rocks!" Be creative.

Next, take a sheet of cardstock or regular copy paper, fold it in half, and then cut along the fold line. After this, simply fold this section in half to make the base for the card.

Now, select a used greeting card that has a picture or image on the front that you want to use for your card. Simply tear out the picture you want for a cool jagged edge effect!

Glue the picture onto the front of your card. Pieces from other cards can also be layered to form a unique look. Finally, use a marker to write your new message inside or on the front.

Ready? Take Five! 5!

guest appearance

Often, the plot of a story will develop through its characters. Their actions, personalities, internal conflicts, and strengths and weaknesses steer the storyline and determine the next sequence of events.

LANGUAGE LINK

plot

LEARNING SETTING

individual

SUPPLIES
Student W.A.L.L.

STANDARDS
Describe how a particular story's or drama's plot unfolds in a series of episodes as well as how the characters respond or change as the plot moves toward a resolution

Introduce a claim(s) and organize the reasons and evidence clearly

CONSIDER YOUR FAVORITE TV SHOW, MOVIE, OR NOVEL. Suddenly, a new character appears out of nowhere—a very unusual character!

Hatchet: As Brian strives to cope in the wilderness following a plane crash with only his hatchet in hand, an old, mystic cave dweller appears.

Star Wars: What if Yoda's wife suddenly entered the scene?

E.T.: The Extra-Terrestrial: Suppose E.T. had a big brother who came to Earth looking for his lost sibling. What if, after finding E.T., this big brother didn't want to leave Earth?

First, select the movie, show, or book. Then describe this unique individual or thing that suddenly enters the picture. How might this new character change the plotline?

Ready? Take Five!

LANGUAGE LINK

graphic organizer

LEARNING SETTING

pair

SUPPLIES
Student W.A.L.L.

STANDARDS
Prepare for and participate effectively in a range of conversations and collaborations with diverse partners, building on others' ideas and expressing their own clearly and persuasively

Write informative/explanatory texts to examine and convey complex ideas and information clearly and accurately through the effective selection, organization, and analysis of content

happy birthday

BIRTHDAYS ARE A SPECIAL TIME—a time for delicious cakes, games, and brightly wrapped packages.

Generally, birthday girls or boys will have no problem expressing their delight as they excitedly tear off the paper. Sometimes, however, it's hard to keep that smile in place when confronted with a pack of notebook paper or underwear.

But you don't want to hurt anyone's feelings, so you grin and give your warmest thank you. In today's task, you and a partner will work together to think of all the best and worst gifts anyone could ever receive. Once selections have been made, place them in an outline form using the following format:

I.   *Best Gifts*
    A.
    B.

II.   *Worst Gifts*
    A.
    B.

Ready? Take Five!

headliners

YOU ARE THE EDITOR OF YOUR TOWN'S NEWSPAPER.
As editor, you have many important decisions
to make. You must be careful to select stories
that will match the interests of your readers.
A good newspaper, however, also has to keep
the public informed of major news events.

Sometimes, those goals come into conflict when the
lead story must be selected. Today is one of those
days. Your reporters have brought four important
stories to your desk. The paper will be printed in a
few short hours, so you don't have long to decide.

Which of the following will you choose to run as
the lead story? Next, explain your choice:

Dog becomes hero, saves baby from burning house

Cargo ship sinks, major water contamination feared

Governor caught in bribery scheme

New factory to open, creates 300 jobs

All are very important. What will you choose and why?

Ready? Take Five!

LANGUAGE LINK

persuasive writing

LEARNING SETTING

individual⁵

SUPPLIES
Student W.A.L.L.

STANDARDS
Write arguments to support
claims with clear reasons and
relevant evidence

reflective writing

individual

SUPPLIES

Student W.A.L.L.

STANDARDS

Develop the topic with relevant facts, definitions, concrete details, quotations, or other information and examples

Use narrative techniques, such as dialogue, pacing, and description, to develop experiences, events, and/or characters

historical interview

CONSIDER A PERSON YOU HAVE STUDIED in history, science, or literature. If you could ask this person four questions, what would those questions be?

Questions cannot be answered with a yes or no response. For instance, you wouldn't want to ask Robert Peary if the North Pole was cold. Duh! You might, however, ask him how he felt when many critics supported someone else's claim to be the first person to reach the North Pole.

Questions need to relate in some way to that individual's accomplishments or career. No answers are necessary.

EXAMPLES

Hercules: What was your hardest labor and why?

Rosa Parks: How did your family feel about the decision you made to stay at the front of the bus?

Dr. Seuss: What were some of the deeper messages you wanted to get across in your stories?

Ready? Take Five!

hometown festival

THE LOCAL OUTDOOR MARKET HAS HIRED YOUR CLASS to help with the upcoming Hometown Festival. All items for sale are locally grown or made. Your team has been assigned to help one vendor. Teams will need to develop catchy, eye-appealing descriptions and slogans to help sell their particular products. But what will your team's vendor be selling?

Think of any item that could be locally produced: a particular vegetable or fruit, honey, handmade baskets, cacti, stained-glass wind chimes, shell necklaces, birdhouses, etc. It's all about your hometown.

Choose your product and then create a flier to distribute to the crowd. Make it as appealing as possible, but make it for your hometown!

Ready? Take Five!

LANGUAGE LINK

setting

LEARNING SETTING

individual[5]

SUPPLIES
Student W.A.L.L.

STANDARDS
Introduce a topic clearly; organize ideas, concepts, and information, using strategies such as definition, classification, comparison/contrast, and cause/ effect; include formatting (e.g., headings), graphics (e.g., charts, tables), and multimedia when useful to aiding comprehension

homegrown poetry 1

FOR HIS POEM, "CONCORD HYMN," American poet (and resident of Concord, MA) Ralph Waldo Emerson, found inspiration in a nearby battlefield where the "shot heard round the world" began the Revolutionary War.

Southern writer Sidney Lanier chose to describe the Chattahoochee River—its ferns, dewberries, and reeds. Christina Rossetti chose the English countryside for her lyric poem, "A Green Cornfield."

Many natural wonders and historic sites have yet to be explored for poetic inspiration. Draw a small dot on your W.A.L.L. This dot represents where you live. Next, draw lines growing out of the dot and label them with local places that could serve as inspiration for a poem.

Is there a lake or stream to the west of you? Was a battle fought nearby or did another historic event take place in your neighborhood? Perhaps you know of a bridge, a bay, an old farmstead, a forest, a valley, an alleyway, or maybe even a train depot or subway.

Place labels at the end of each of these lines.

Ready? Take Five! 5!

Gulf of Mexico

Camp Helen

St. Andrews Bay

Zoo World

Frank Brown Park

homegrown poetry 2

FOR TODAY'S TAKE FIVE, SELECT ONE OF THE PLACES MARKED on your map in Homegrown Poetry I.

Next, make a list of sensory details associated with your selected location—details that develop the flavor of the place (its sights, smells, and sounds) and possibly reveal a truth or new idea to the reader.

Think of all the senses as you make your list.

Ready? Take Five! **5!**

LANGUAGE LINK

poetry

LEARNING SETTING

individual[5]

SUPPLIES
Student W.A.L.L.

STANDARDS
Use precise words and phrases, relevant descriptive details, and sensory language to convey experiences and events

LANGUAGE LINK
poetry

LEARNING SETTING
individual⁵

SUPPLIES
Student W.A.L.L.

STANDARDS
Analyze the structure of texts, including how specific sentences, paragraphs, and larger portions of the text (e.g., a section, chapter, scene, or stanza) relate to each other and the whole

Produce clear and coherent writing in which the development, organization, and style are appropriate to task, purpose, and audience

homegrown poetry 3

In poetry, stanzas divide a poem into units, or groups of lines. Often, they have a specific rhyme scheme or meter.

USING THE DETAILS IN THE PREVIOUS TAKE FIVE, pull these images together to form a short poem of at least two stanzas, one that expresses a special idea or truth.

Ready? Take Five!

in search of . . .

YEARS AGO, A POPULAR TELEVISION SHOW called *In Search Of . . .* entertained audiences with unusual "searches" each week. On one episode, they searched for mummies and on another, UFOs.

Each week, you would find them combing the globe for strange creatures, pirate treasure, Big Foot, the Loch Ness Monster, or the plane of Amelia Earhart, along with a wide assortment of other unusual people, places, and events.

The program has once again been revived (brought back to life). A major network will be airing this show each Monday, and you have been hired to create its first two episodes.

What will you be *In Search Of . . .* ? Where will you go, and what do you hope to find? Write the name of each program along with a promotion of the upcoming show.

Ready? Take Five!

LANGUAGE LINK

creative writing

LEARNING SETTING

pair[5]

SUPPLIES
Student W.A.L.L.

STANDARDS

Develop the topic with relevant facts, definitions, concrete details, quotations, or other information and examples

Include multimedia components (e.g., graphic, images, music, sound) and visual displays in presentations to clarify information

TEACHER TIP

Students can take their places behind and in front of the cameras as they produce their own *In Search Of . . .* based on their responses to the prompt, selecting the best ones, dividing into teams, conducting the research, and then moving from storyboarding to filming.

LANGUAGE LINK
myths

LEARNING SETTING
individual

SUPPLIES
Plain paper or construction paper

STANDARDS
Interpret figures of speech (e.g., literary, biblical, and mythological allusions) in context

Use narrative techniques, such as dialogue, pacing, and description, to develop experiences, events, and/or characters

TEACHER TIP
Students will enjoy testing their powers of observation as they try to identify the constellation in the night sky at Kids Astronomy (**www.kidsastronomy.com/ astroskymap/constellation _hunt.htm**).

in the stars

Myths are legendary stories, often depicting gods and goddesses and other superhuman beings. Many offer imaginary explanations for natural events.

A BULL, A SCORPION, AN ARCHER, A LION—these figures and many more live in the heavens with their myths and legends created long, long ago. One popular story surrounds the constellation of Cancer, the Crab.

The great Hercules was in a fierce battle with the multi-headed serpent, Hydra. Watching the battle was his enemy, Hera, who was cheering for Hydra. Hera was determined that Hercules would not win. She decided to send a crab to distract him. Annoyed at the creature biting at his ankles, Hercules kicked the crab all the way into the heavens; thus, Cancer was born.

Your task today is to create a new constellation. On your paper, arrange a series of dots to represent your figure. Next, use your pencil to lightly connect the dots. Beneath your creation, write the name of the constellation and a brief story about its creation.

Ready? Take Five!

inventive vocabulary 1

OPENING THE DICTIONARY, YOU FLIP TO A PAGE with the heading, "festive-fib." The heading means that this page includes all of the words that fall alphabetically between the words "festive" and "fib." Running your finger down the page, you finally arrive at the word you need. What is that word?

Your task is to create a new word that will fit between the words in the heading somewhere on that page. Use a dictionary to help you add the next parts of this challenge.

Provide its definition, its part of speech, and any other information that will help readers who stumble upon this new word.

Ready? Take Five! **5!**

LANGUAGE LINK
reference materials

LEARNING SETTING
individual

SUPPLIES
Student W.A.L.L.

Dictionary

STANDARDS
Determine or clarify the meaning of unknown and multiple-meaning words and phrases by using context clues, analyzing meaningful word parts, and consulting general and specialized reference materials, as appropriate

TEACHER TIP
This prompt can be repeated periodically using different guide words from the dictionary.

When it comes to learning real words, however, a site not to be missed is the Visuwords website. One word suddenly multiplies into its many parts—synonyms, antonyms, etc. This online graphical dictionary can be found at **www.visuwords.com**.

reference materials

individual

SUPPLIES

Student W.A.L.L.

Dictionary

STANDARDS

Determine or clarify the meaning of unknown and multiple-meaning words and phrases by using context clues, analyzing meaningful word parts, and consulting general and specialized reference materials, as appropriate

inventive vocabulary 2

ONCE AGAIN, YOU ARE SEARCHING THE DICTIONARY for just the right word for your story. This time, you stop at the page heading, "buttonhole–bystander." What is this new and unusual word? What part of speech is it, and what is the definition? Finally, use the new word in a sentence.

Ready? Take Five!

invitation only

LOOK WHO'S HAVING A BIRTHDAY PARTY! It's a character from one of our favorite stories.

We just received the invitation in the mail. Examine it closely. Notice how the design, wording, colors, and fonts reflect this character.

In pairs, consider a popular character (e.g., Robin Hood, Ron Weasley, Babe the pig, Bella Swan, Little Red Riding Hood) or select someone from a book you recently read in class such as Jonas from *The Giver*. How might the invitation appear?

Your task is to use the materials provided to create a birthday invitation that represents this character. Robin Hood's invitation, for instance, might be in the shape of a tree that opens in the middle; the message is hidden inside, just like Robin Hood hides in Sherwood Forest.

Does the invitation ask guests to bring something special? Does it mention specific entertainment or food? Get the idea?

Ready? Take Five! 5!

SUPPLIES

Construction paper or card stock

Markers

Scissors

Glue

An assortment of scrapbooking supplies (scissors, punch)

Desktop publishing software (opt.)

STANDARDS

Analyze how particular elements of a story or drama interact (e.g., how setting shapes the characters or plot)

Include multimedia components (e.g., graphics, images, music, sound) and visual displays in presentations to clarify information

LANGUAGE LINK

characterization

LEARNING SETTING

collaboration

SUPPLIES

Plain and construction paper

Scissors

Glue

Markers

Desktop publishing software (opt.)

STANDARDS

Include multimedia components (e.g., graphics, images, music, sound) and visual displays in presentations to clarify information

Analyze in detail how a key individual, event, or idea is introduced, illustrated, and elaborated in a text (e.g., through examples or anecdotes)

TEACHER TIP

Janet and Allan Ahlberg's *The Jolly Postman* makes a wonderful introduction to this prompt with invitations, advertising flyers, and other types of mail sent to notable fairytale characters. An extension for this prompt could be used following the reading of a novel where students then create mail for characters they have studied.

junk mail

ON RETURNING HOME FROM VACATION, you find a large stack of mail built up in your mailbox. Everything from credit card offers to sales brochures have found their way to your home. Looking randomly through each envelope, you see nothing unusual. Someone else, however, might find an accurate description of you by the mail you receive.

For this task, a select stash of mail will be created to define a fictional character of your choosing. It should represent his or her personality, interests, friends, job, or lifestyle.

Mickey Mouse, for example, might have an invitation to a cheese tasting, a package of extra shiny black shoe polish, or a travel agency flier with a special discount on any Disney excursion.

The challenge for your team is to make a list of at least three items found in the character's mailbox, delegate tasks, and then use the materials available to create your individual's mail.

Ready? Take Five!

keep it green 1

REUSE AND RECYCLE—THESE ARE TWO OF THE BEST WAYS to help our planet stay green. Unfortunately, millions of pounds of plastic bottles still make it to the landfill each year. Besides reusing bottles that are safe enough to be refilled with water, what else can be done with these plastic nuisances?

Teams should grab a piece of chart paper and a marker to list as many different ideas as possible. Lists should then be posted together so the teams can share their responses.

Ready? Take Five! **5!**

LANGUAGE LINK
problem solving

LEARNING SETTING
collaboration

SUPPLIES
Chart paper or newsprint

STANDARDS
Develop the topic with relevant facts, definitions, concrete details, quotations, or other information and examples

Prepare for and participate effectively in a range of conversations and collaborations with diverse partners, building on others' ideas and expressing their own clearly and persuasively

TEACHER TIP
An interesting video that follows the complete life cycle of a plastic bottle is "My Life as a Plastic Bottle" on YouTube: **www.youtube.com/watch?v=J112v94mcho**.

SUPPLIES
Plastic bottles

String

Scissors

Construction paper

Assorted craft items (rubber bands, paperclips, hooks, etc.)

STANDARDS
Include multimedia components (e.g., graphics, images, music, sound) and visual displays in presentations to clarify information

TEACHER TIP
Some bottles may be cut in half ahead of time. These partial bottles may present different ideas for reuse.

keep it green 2

IN TODAY'S TAKE FIVE, REVIEW THE IDEAS presented for new and improved uses for plastic bottles. Use one of these ideas (or an entirely different concept) to transform a common plastic bottle into another useful item, going beyond the usual vase of flowers. The most creative products can be selected to create a display in a visible location in the school.

Ready? Take Five!

klonzo 1

LINES ARE GROWING LONG OUTSIDE the local department store, and it's still thirty minutes from opening. The crowd is growing impatient. Why are they here? It seems that word has leaked out that a new shipment of "klonzo" has arrived.

Now that last year's "plicklets" are out of style, everyone wants to claim his or her very own "klonzo." Wait a minute! Klonzo? What is everyone talking about? Is it a new toy or a piece of technology? A unique car or perhaps a revolutionary shoe?

You decide, and then convince us to buy one as well.

Ready? Take Five! 🄻

LANGUAGE LINK

persuasive writing

LEARNING SETTING

individual

SUPPLIES
Student W.A.L.L.

STANDARDS
Support claim(s) with clear reasons and relevant evidence, using credible sources and demonstrating an understanding of the topic or text

LANGUAGE LINK

persuasive writing

LEARNING SETTING

individual

SUPPLIES

Plain paper

Markers

Samples of magazine and newspaper ads

Desktop publishing software (opt.)

STANDARDS

Include multimedia components (e.g., graphics, images, music, sound) and visual displays in presentations to clarify information

TEACHER TIP

A beginner's activity for advertising production can be found at the PBS Kids' webpage, "Create Your Own Ad," found at **www.pbskids.org/ dontbuyit/advertisingtricks/ createyourownad_flash.html**.

A more comprehensive study of advertising that includes activities can be found at TeachingKidsBusiness.com (**www.teachingkidsbusiness .com**).

klonzo 2

USE THE PREVIOUS TAKE FIVE TO DEVELOP AN ADVERTISEMENT for this popular item. Create a newspaper or magazine ad that will be sure to increase klonzo sales even more!

Ready? Take Five! **5!**

law makers

Jargon is that language that confines itself to a particular workplace. When mechanics speak of a "tune up" and lawyers speak of the "party of the first part," they are using their specialized vocabulary-jargon.

IN MANY STATES, IT'S NOW AGAINST THE LAW TO TEXT while driving. Some states require motorcyclists to wear helmets. But did you know that it's also illegal to carry skunks into Tennessee? And don't even think about spitting on a bus in Washington. In New Jersey, be sure to smile at police officers; you could be breaking the law by simply frowning in their direction.

These outdated laws are rarely enforced; they just haven't been taken off the books. Many were initially passed in an effort to keep citizens morally upright and honest. To most people today, they seem silly when compared to current behavioral standards.

You and your fellow legislators, however, feel that enough is enough! It's time to get tough once again. Select two seemingly innocent actions. Create a law for each that will make such actions illegal. Don't forget the legal jargon!

Ready? Take Five!

LANGUAGE LINK

words and phrases

LEARNING SETTING

pair⁵

SUPPLIES
Student W.A.L.L.

STANDARDS
Use precise language and domain-specific vocabulary to inform about or explain the topic

Adapt speech to a variety of contexts and communicative tasks, demonstrating command of formal English when indicated or appropriate

SUPPLIES
Student W.A.L.L.

STANDARDS
Write informative/explanatory texts to examine and convey complex ideas and information clearly and accurately through the effective selection, organization, and analysis of content

Use appropriate transitions to clarify the relationships among ideas and concepts

TEACHER TIP
A wonderful little book to accompany this activity that students of all ages will enjoy is *The Giving Tree* by Shel Silverstein.

learning tree

ARBOR DAY IS A DAY WHEN TREES BECOME THE CENTER of attention. Many people celebrate Arbor Day by planting a tree. Some people like to pay tribute to someone they love and respect by planting a tree in their honor. Others plant a tree in someone's memory.

Planting a tree, however, takes effort. First, you must wait until the right time of the year, usually the cool months of fall or winter. Next, you have to dig a hole at least three times wider than the root ball of the tree. Place the tree into the hole, cover it with dirt and mulch, and water it frequently. These directions, however, are for regular trees.

Your task today is to provide a list of instructions for planting and nourishing an entirely different kind of tree: a learning tree, also known as the Tree of Knowledge. How would you plant it and care for it? Does it produce a type of bloom, flower, or fruit? If so, describe it. Does it undergo a change from one season to the next?

Take all of these things into consideration as you describe the process of planting and nurturing a learning tree.

Ready? Take Five!

lemonade stand

LEMONADE FOR SALE! Customers have been steady this morning at Alex's lemonade stand. He has already made more than six dollars. Things are going much better than last week when he barely made two dollars for the entire day!

What has made the difference? First, he changed the name on his poster from "Lemonade Stand" to "Alex's Lemon Squeeze." This immediately gave his stand more curb appeal.

Next, he developed a new strategy. On the poster he added, "Ten cents of all sales go to the Humane Society," which is one of his favorite causes. Looking ahead to next week, he has decided to make his sales promotion all about the hot temperatures: "Ninety degrees and melting. Time to chill."

Today's task is to create your own lemonade stand. Provide a catchy name, a promotional slogan, and a strategy that will be certain to boost your sales.

Ready? Take Five! **5!**

LANGUAGE LINK

persuasive writing

LEARNING SETTING

individual

SUPPLIES

Markers

Construction paper strips

Desktop publishing software (opt.)

STANDARDS

Use precise words and phrases, relevant descriptive details, and sensory language to convey experiences and events

Distinguish among the connotations (associations) of words with similar denotations (definitions) (e.g., stingy, scrimpy, economical, unwasteful, thrifty)

TEACHER TIP

A perfect inspiration for this prompt would be pitchers of ice-cold lemonade to help boost descriptive taste buds!

SUPPLIES

Atlas

Maps

Student W.A.L.L.

STANDARDS

Develop the topic with relevant facts, definitions, concrete details, quotations, or other information and examples

Determine or clarify the meaning of unknown and multiple-meaning words and phrases by using context clues, analyzing meaningful word parts, and consulting general and specialized reference materials, as appropriate

TEACHER TIP

A digital extension for this prompt would be to let your students use Google Maps (**www.maps.google.com**) or MapQuest (**www.mapquest .com**) to zoom in on and discover new cities and towns.

loony town

IF YOU WERE TO COMBINE THE NAMES Arkansas and Philadelphia, you would get Arkadelphia, an actual town in Alabama. As new towns and communities keep popping up across America, names are in short supply. After all, you can only have so many Springvilles, Troys, and Centervilles.

The task for today is to combine the names of two or three existing cities or towns for a completely new name. Then, provide a brief description of the town based on the new name.

For example, what could you get if you combined Topeka, Kansas, and Yuma, Arizona? Kanyumatop—population: 3,400; major industry: the recycling of tabs from aluminum cans.

The study of place names, by the way, is called toponymy, so this prompt would make you a toponymyist.

Ready? Take Five!

lost

Tone refers to the writer's attitude toward his or her story. The writer's tone sets the mood or atmosphere for the story with carefully selected words, phrases, and details. Often, the tone will change as events change.

AS THE TRAIL LOOPS BACK TO THE EAST, the hikers start to feel the miles in their tired muscles. For five hours, they have trekked along a winding trail in the Great Smoky Mountains, located in eastern Tennessee. Occasionally, a member of the group pauses to take a long sip from his water bottle, but other than that, they keep walking.

By five o'clock, the sun lazily hovers above a ridge in the distance. Though not in a rush, they know they will need to make camp soon. Ted, in the lead, turns to signal to the others, but something seems out of place. Puzzled, he begins counting . . . one, two, three, four, five. Odd—there should be six of them. Peering into the distance, he looks farther down the trail, but no one is there. The others turn, and the realization dawns on them as well. Where is Adam?

Only you can answer this question as you complete the short story, "The Smoky Mountain Hikers." Shift the tone in another direction as well.

Ready? Take Five! **5!**

LANGUAGE LINK

tone

LEARNING SETTING

individual

SUPPLIES
Student W.A.L.L.

STANDARDS
Interpret words and phrases as they are used in a text, including determining technical, connotative, and figurative meanings, and analyze how specific word choices shape meaning or tone

Provide a conclusion that follows from and reflects on the narrated experiences and events

TEACHER TIP

Students can create a representation of this creative-thinking activity for another Take Five using sample materials, bags, or an assortment of objects.

A class project could involve writing a letter to a major company explaining the idea and sending a few of the class samples.

make that a tween meal to go

FOR KIDS LIKE WILL AND TRACY, fast-food restaurants are always a hit, especially when they offer small-sized meals in a bag or box. Along with their burgers and fries, young customers might also receive a toy from the latest movie or perhaps a game, sticker, or other small item.

Unfortunately for their older sister, Sherry, no specially designed packages are available for people her age. Even at the age of fourteen, she orders the kids meal but quickly tosses the extras to her brother and sister. Those who are twelve and older have been overlooked in the fast-food market. That is, until now.

Your challenge is to list as many different age-appropriate items that might go into a tween or teen meal. Items need to be sized so they fit easily and conveniently into a lunch bag-sized container.

For example, a single from an album that a recording artist wants to promote, a Sudoku puzzle, or maybe a colorful gel pen and tiny writing tablet—the possibilities are endless. Remember, all items must be parent friendly.

Ready? Take Five!

mind travelers

IN THE BOOK *SLAUGHTERHOUSE-FIVE*, Billy Pilgrim was always on the road—mentally. One moment, he might be in a prisoner-of-war camp during World War II; in the next scene, he might be on the alien planet of Tralfamadore.

If confronted with a painful memory or uncomfortable situation, he might suddenly open his eyes and find himself in the 1950s or 1960s. This sudden switching from one place to the next was the author's way of showing, rather than merely describing to the reader, the confusion of this main character.

What if you had that ability? For example, say you pick up your pencil to begin a test and immediately regret that you did not study the night before. Where would you go if you could close your eyes and take off? Explain where you are, the time period, and what you are doing.

Ready? Take Five! 5!

LANGUAGE LINK

expository writing

LEARNING SETTING

individual⁵

SUPPLIES
Student W.A.L.L.

STANDARDS
Develop the topic with relevant, well-chosen facts, definitions, concrete details, quotations, or other information and examples

Explain how an author develops the point of view of the narrator or speaker in a text

Analyze how a text makes connections among and distinctions between individual, ideas, or events (e.g., through comparisons, analogies, or categories)

SUPPLIES
Simple props for each team

STANDARDS
Pose and respond to specific questions with elaboration and detail by making comments that contribute to the topic, text, or issue under discussion

Determine or clarify the meaning of unknown and multiple-meaning words and phrases by using context clues, analyzing meaningful word parts, and consulting general and specialized reference materials, as appropriate

Present claims and findings, sequencing ideas logically and using pertinent description, facts, and details to accentuate main ideas or themes; use appropriate eye contact, adequate volume, and clear pronunciation

TEACHER TIP
Writing isn't the only form of communication. Today's challenge requires each group to develop a short skit to demonstrate examples related to the topic of etiquette. Skits may be performed for the next day's Take Five activity, during an extension of today's Take Five, or at the end of class.

mind your manners

THE WORD *ETIQUETTE* MEANS A SET OF BEHAVIORS that people use to show good manners. Because of etiquette, people use forks and knives when they eat steak instead of their fingers. They also send thank-you notes for gifts they have received–even that striped red and green sweater that Grandmother Thelma knitted.

The manners practiced today, however, may be very different from those used by cavemen, desert nomads, cannibals, or knights in armor.

In today's task, each team will select a particular group of people and then create three rules of etiquette for them. Instead of writing the rule down, however, each group will create a brief skit demonstrating the use of this rule.

Ready? Take Five!

mirror, mirror on the wall

LANGUAGE LINK
reflective writing

LEARNING SETTING
individual

SUPPLIES
Student W.A.L.L.

STANDARDS
Draw evidence from literary or informational texts to support analysis, reflection, and research

SNOW WHITE'S ANTAGONIST UTTERED THESE WORDS, thinking that she, of course, was the "fairest of them all." Was she ever wrong!

Many character lessons and activities ask students to reflect on the following question: How do others view you? These lessons are designed to show how our actions and words reveal more about ourselves than what we may desire. Many people might answer that others see them as a good friend, someone with a pleasant personality, or a caring person who is funny or artistic.

That, however, isn't the objective of this Take Five. Instead, today's challenge is to consider how you would *not* want to be viewed by others. Would it be a person who is bossy or always late? What about someone who can never make a decision—in other words, wishy-washy?

For this task, you will make a list of four traits that you do not want to possess—those you definitely do *not* want attached to you.

Ready? Take Five! 5!

SUPPLIES

Student W.A.L.L.

STANDARDS

Use precise words and phrases, telling details, and sensory language to convey a vivid picture of the experiences, events, setting, and/or characters

TEACHER TIP

This two-part Take Five activity could be attached to an independent reading unit that features animals:

Black Horses for the King
—Anne McCaffrey

The Call of the Wild
—Jack London

Hoot
—Carl Hiaasen

Lassie Come Home
—Eric Knight

The Music of Dolphins
—Karen Hesse

No More Dead Dogs
—Gordon Korman

Old Yeller
—Fred Gipson

Skin Deep
—E.M. Crane

Where the Red Fern Grows
—Wilson Rawls

The Yearling
—Marjorie Kinnan Rawlings

missing pet 1

OH DEAR! A VERY SPECIAL PET HAS GONE MISSING. Everyone in the neighborhood is teaming up to help find the missing animal. Your team is in charge of making fliers to post around the neighborhood. The first decision is the most obvious—who is missing?

Brainstorm a list of famous pets from cartoons, books, or movies. Maybe it's Scooby-Doo, the Cheshire Cat, Brian Griffin, Snoopy, or Garfield? Next, think of all the different character traits of the pet, such as notable markings, features, and behavior.

Ready? Take Five!

missing pet 2

IT'S TIME TO ADD THE NEXT STEP—COMMUNICATION—as your team pulls all its ideas together from the previous Take Five to create a very visible, well-designed flier to post around town. Be as specific as possible if you want someone to find this unique pet.

Ready? Take Five! 5!

SUPPLIES

Markers

Plain paper

Desktop publishing software program (opt.)

STANDARDS

Make strategic use of digital media (e.g., textual, graphical, audio, visual, and interactive elements) in presentations to enhance understanding of findings, reasoning, and evidence and to add interest

Demonstrate command of the conventions of standard English capitalization, punctuation, and spelling when writing

SUPPLIES PER TEAM

    3 straws

    4 pipe cleaners

    1 coat hanger

    10 paperclips

    Geometric shapes of
    construction paper

    Cotton balls

    Pieces of string or ribbon

STANDARDS

Include multimedia components (e.g., graphics, images, music, sound) and visual displays in presentation to clarify information

Prepare for and participate effectively in a range of conversations and collaborations with diverse partners, building on others' ideas and expressing their own clearly and persuasively

TEACHER TIP

Though some items may be substituted, the geometric shapes are essential. When complete, mobiles may be displayed around the classroom or school.

For this challenge, pictures of Alexander Calder's famous mobiles would be interesting to view. These can be seen at the Calder Foundation website (**www.calder.org**).

Create an interactive mobile at the NGAkids Art Zone (**www.nga. gov/kids/zone/zone.htm**). Here, students can make changes and add branches, shapes, and colors to the mobile on screen. They can also put it into motion.

mobile art 1

WHEN YOU HEAR THE WORD "MOBILE," most people think of cute animal shapes that dangle over a baby's crib. Famous American artist Alexander Calder, however, created this suspended art form. Today, Calder's works hang in museums all over the world and sell for thousands of dollars. Viewers can see firsthand the geometrical shapes that dangle from many of his works of art.

Today you will begin creating your own Calder-style mobile using the supplies provided. All members will work on different sections of the mobile.

Ready? Take Five! **5!**

mobile art 2

TODAY'S TAKE FIVE CHALLENGE IS TO CONNECT the sections and attach them to make one hanging mobile. These can be displayed by hanging them from the ceiling or above a window.

Ready? Take Five! **5!**

LANGUAGE LINK
problem solving

LEARNING SETTING
collaboration

SUPPLIES PER TEAM

 3 straws
 4 pipe cleaners
 1 coat hanger
 10 paperclips
 Geometric shapes of construction paper
 Cotton balls
 Pieces of string or ribbon

STANDARDS

Include multimedia components (e.g., graphics, images, music, sound) and visual displays in presentation to clarify information

Prepare for and participate effectively in a range of conversations and collaborations with diverse partners, building on others' ideas and expressing their own clearly and persuasively

persuasive writing

individual

SUPPLIES

Student W.A.L.L.

STANDARDS

Introduce claim(s) with clear reasons and relevant evidence, using credible sources and demonstrating an understanding of the topic or text

TEACHER TIP

Students will enjoy seeing the American Film Institute's list of 100 greatest movies ever made at **www.afi.com/100years/ movies10.aspx**.

movie critic

When developing an argument, writers should keep in mind counterarguments made by those who oppose their ideas. By addressing these directly and providing logical reasons against them, writers strengthen their own arguments.

IN A RECENT SURVEY, THE MOVIES *AVATAR*, *Gone with the Wind*, and *Star Wars* were selected as three of the most popular movies of all time. Did anyone ask you? Then it's time to voice your opinion.

In today's challenge, you will write a persuasive argument to support your pick for "most popular of all time." Choose from one of these categories: movies, YouTube videos, musicians, and video or board games.

Be sure to include specific evidence: "It was funny; I laughed a lot," or "It had lots of blood!" Sorry, those reasons could apply to too many movies or video games. What makes your selection the absolute best? You must provide specific, convincing evidence that this is the best of all time.

Ready? Take Five! 5!

movie editor

MOST MOVIES HAVE MANY SCENES THAT NEVER MAKE IT to the big screen due to the work of film editors. For instance, did you know that tough guy actor Harrison Ford, who starred in such franchises as "Star Wars" (Han Solo) and "Indiana Jones", also played a school principal in the movie *E.T.: The Extra-Terrestrial*? Probably not, since that scene was left out of the final version of the film.

In today's challenge, you and a partner will pair up to select an important scene from any popular movie and cut it from the final product.

Suppose, for instance, that Helen/Elastigirl from *The Incredibles* did not have the power to stretch herself in the scene involving the plane crash. How would that have changed the outcome of the story? What if Harry had not won the first task in *Harry Potter and the Goblet of Fire*?

Select the scene and then describe how this omission would have affected the plot and the characters.

Ready? Take Five! **5!**

LANGUAGE LINK

plot development

LEARNING SETTING

pair[5]

SUPPLIES
Student W.A.L.L.

STANDARDS
Analyze how particular lines of dialogue or incidents in a story or drama propel the action, reveal aspects of a character, or provoke a decision

Analyze how an author's choices concerning how to structure specific parts of a text (e.g., the choice of where to begin or end a story, the choice to provide a comedic or tragic resolution) contribute to its overall structure and meaning as well as its aesthetic impact

LANGUAGE LINK

parts of speech

LEARNING SETTING

pair

SUPPLIES

Two containers, one filled with slips of paper on which a noun is written, the other with active verbs

STANDARDS

Use vivid words and phrases, telling details, and sensory language to convey a vivid picture of the experiences, events, setting, and/or characters

Vary sentence patterns for meaning, reader/listener interest, and style

Demonstrate command of the conventions of standard English grammar and usage when writing or speaking

movie madness

Active verbs tell what action someone or something is performing, physically or mentally. They add crispness and energy to writing. For example, "He is afraid of the dark," can be changed to, "The dark frightens him."

THE CARROT THAT ATE CALIFORNIA! Now there's a movie waiting to be made. Today's challenge is to create a strong title for the next blockbuster movie.

In one container are slips of paper with a noun written on each. In a second container are slips of paper with an active verb on each.

One partner will pull a noun slip; the other will pull a verb slip. Next, put the words together to create the most fascinating title ever!

EXAMPLES

"Cave" and "Revolt" = The Bloody Revolt of Vampire Cave Dwellers
"Bus" and "Eat" = The Monster Frog That Eats School Buses

Any form of the word may be used.

Ready? Take Five!

name game

When people text each other, much can be said with only a few letters. Acronyms such as LOL (laughing out loud) use the first letter of each word to represent a thought or idea. For this challenge, however, only complete sentences may be used. That means that every group of words must form a complete thought and have a subject (or an understood subject) and a verb.

AMY HAS JUST DISCOVERED SOMETHING INTERESTING. If she takes each letter of her name, she can make a sentence "**A**dd **M**ore **Y**ellow." This is the Acronym Game, in which each first letter of a name is used as a separate word.

In this game, however, the words must make a complete sentence. Amy also could have created "**A**sk **M**y **Y**ak" or "**A**unt **M**aggie **Y**awned." Even if your name is Cy you can still participate in this task: "**C**hris **Y**odeled."

In this task, you will use your name as an acronym to develop at least three sentences.

Ready? Take Five!

LANGUAGE LINK

sentence structure

LEARNING SETTING

individual

SUPPLIES
Student W.A.L.L.

STANDARDS
Demonstrate command of the conventions of standard English grammar and usage when writing or speaking

Develop the topic with relevant facts, definitions, concrete details, quotations or other information and examples

TEACHER TIP
This activity can be used multiple times when the prompt is changed: last names, favorite sports teams, hometowns, favorite colors, etc.

LANGUAGE LINK
imagery

LEARNING SETTING
individual

SUPPLIES
Student W.A.L.L.

STANDARDS
Analyze the structure of texts, including how specific sentences, paragraphs, and larger portions of the text (e.g., a section, chapter, scene, or stanza) relate to each other and the whole

Use precise words and phrases, relevant descriptive details, and sensory language to convey experiences and events

natural haiku

Haiku poetry combines a series of images to make a visual impact on the reader. Traditional haiku poems use a set number of syllables per line: five syllables in the first line, seven in the second, and five in the last line.

YOU ARE WALKING ALONG THE BAY AND SUDDENLY a mullet, a common saltwater fish, leaps from the water and lands with a loud *ka-splash*. Your mind starts to wander.

"Above the waters" you mentally begin writing. Okay, that sounds good, and it's five syllables. In fact, it sounds like a haiku in progress. "A leaping fish lands ka-splash." That makes seven syllables. One more line to go. "The quiet returns." That's five syllables, a complete haiku.

Let's try that again. Select one object from nature and place it in its natural world, doing what it does . . . naturally. Some examples include a honeybee pollinating a blossom, a beaver building a dam, a dog chewing a bone, a shark circling its prey, etc.

There are so many possibilities! Select one to create a new three-line haiku.

Ready? Take Five!

newspaper editor

Euphemisms are words and phrases that tactfully skirt the truth. These words and phrases replace other words that might be offensive or insensitive. Instead of saying someone has died, we say that they have passed away. With euphemisms, being fired becomes being "let go" and a lie becomes "bending the truth."

HOW CAN YOU BE HONEST WITHOUT HURTING anyone's feelings? Euphemisms! They work like this:

Mom: "Did you enjoy the tuna casserole?"

You: "Uh, it was like savoring the taste of the sea."

As editor of your school newspaper, *The Hook*, it is your responsibility to cover all major events associated with the school: sports, clubs, awards, special activities, etc. You are not, however, looking forward to the current task–writing a review of the drama club's latest play for the entertainment section. It was their version of *High School Musical* with acting, dancing, and singing. The problem? It was bad—really bad—and the people in the play are your good friends.

Now it's time to write that review. Use your best euphemisms to describe the play: the acting, dancing, and—whew!—singing.

Ready? Take Five! 5!

LANGUAGE LINK

words and phrases

LEARNING SETTING

collaboration

SUPPLIES
Student W.A.L.L.

STANDARDS
Interpret figures of speech (e.g., euphemism, oxymoron) in context and analyze their role in the text

Produce clear and coherent writing in which the development, organization, and style are appropriate to task, purpose, and audience

author's purpose

individual

SUPPLIES
Student W.A.L.L.

STANDARDS
Assess how point of view or purpose shapes the content and style of a text

Develop the topic with relevant facts, definitions, concrete details, quotations, or other information and examples

the next kid/ teen chef

DUE TO THE POPULARITY OF COOKING PROGRAMS such as *The Next Food Network Star* and *Top Chef,* people of all ages are finding themselves in the kitchen. These programs target a specific audience: people who have little time in the kitchen, enjoy backyard barbecues, like to entertain, or can't get enough of Southern or Italian food. These chefs bring to the television screen their particular points of view.

The Food Network is currently searching for its next cooking star—a much younger chef who can connect with the sixteen and under market. Could you be that star? First, decide on your show's focus: afterschool snacks, bite-sized babysitting munchies, lunches for gaming junkies, or something else entirely?

Next, make a list of the foods that will be featured on your first episode. Typically, each show highlights at least three different dishes. Let your imagination and taste buds lead the way.

Ready? Take Five!

no bully zone

UH OH! THE SCHOOL BULLY IS HEADING YOUR WAY down the hall. Sure, you may be tall and strong, but this bully just likes to pick on everybody. It's not worth taking a risk and getting into trouble. Avoid confrontation! Think fast!

Without using physical violence or abusive language, list three creative ways to get past the oncoming bully.

Ready? Take Five! 5!

LANGUAGE LINK

conflict

LEARNING SETTING

individual

SUPPLIES
Student W.A.L.L.

STANDARDS
Analyze the interactions between individuals, events, and ideas in a text (e.g., how ideas influence individuals or events, or how individuals influence ideas or events)

Develop the topic with relevant facts, definitions, concrete details, quotations, or other information and examples

problem solving

pair

SUPPLIES

Student W.A.L.L.

Foam noodles, cut into
two-foot sections

STANDARDS

Prepare for and participate
effectively in a range of
conversations and collaborations
with diverse partners, building on
others' ideas and expressing their
own clearly and persuasively

Support claim(s) with clear
reasons and relevant evidence,
using credible sources and
demonstrating an understanding
of the topic or text

noodle mania 1

NOODLES SEEM TO BE EVERYWHERE! Though they were once
used in spaghetti and swimming pools, now there are
oodles of uses for long (and short) foam noodles. One
popular game show even allows people to win money by
dropping small marbles down a noodle's hollow center
to try and knock over plastic bottles. Many seamstresses
and clothing designers wrap cloth around the noodles
to prevent wrinkling. Kids can use them for sword fights
or hockey sticks. Some people have even cut off a small
section to rest their heads on when soaking in a hot
bathtub. Now it's your turn. With a partner, list many,
unique ways to use a foam noodle.

Ready? Take Five!

noodle mania 2

FOR TODAY'S TAKE FIVE, you and your partner will review the list made in the previous Take Five and select the one that seems most unique. Use the foam noodle section to create your idea.

Ready? Take Five!

LANGUAGE LINK

problem solving

LEARNING SETTING

pair

SUPPLIES

Student W.A.L.L.

Foam noodles, cut into two-foot sections

STANDARDS

Prepare for and participate effectively in a range of conversations and collaborations with diverse partners, building on others' ideas and expressing their own clearly and persuasively

Support claim(s) with clear reasons and relevant evidence, using credible sources and demonstrating an understanding of the topic or text

TEACHER TIP

This can be taken one step further by allowing each team to make an advertisement for its product (e.g., newspaper ad, Internet pop-up, infomercial).

LANGUAGE LINK

persuasive writing

LEARNING SETTING

collaboration

SUPPLIES
Student W.A.L.L.

STANDARDS
Introduce claim(s) and organize the reasons and evidence clearly

TEACHER TIP
A wide variety of PSAs can be selected for an appropriate audience from the Ad Council's website: **www.adcouncil.org**

Among the PSA topics are bullying, staying in school, and the risks of drinking and driving.

now hear this! 1

Public Service Announcements (PSAs) are frequently heard on radio and television. Organizations use PSAs to get their message across to the public.

THE AMERICAN CANCER SOCIETY PROMOTES its annual Relay for Life by persuading people to walk for the cure. Celebrities often remind students to stay in school or avoid drugs. PSAs are used to help make the world a better place. Imagine if these announcements could be made by an important person from the past! Your task is to decide what will be your PSA and who will be the best person for this task. Then write a thirty-second skit for a PSA. Tomorrow's Take Five will give each team the opportunity to rehearse its PSA.

Ready? Take Five!

now hear this! 2

READY! SET! ACTION! LET THE PSAS BEGIN! Each group will perform the PSA created in the previous Take Five to the class or rehearse the PSA in preparation for a later performance of the final product.

Ready? Take Five!

LANGUAGE LINK

persuasive writing

LEARNING SETTING

collaboration

SUPPLIES

Student W.A.L.L.

STANDARDS

Introduce claim(s) and organize the reasons and evidence clearly

---

TEACHER TIP

This activity can be expanded by allowing students to film their PSAS. Final products can be edited with programs such as Windows Live Movie Maker or Apple's iMovie.

Consider posting the best submissions on YouTube or playing them during a school news broadcast.

parts of speech

individual[5]

SUPPLIES

Student W.A.L.L.

STANDARDS

Demonstrate command of the conventions of standard English grammar and usage when writing or speaking

Introduce a topic; organize ideas, concepts, and information, using strategies such as definition, classification, comparison/contrast, and cause/effect; include formatting (e.g., headings), graphic (e.g., charts, tables), and multimedia when useful to aiding comprehension

numbed to the max

To tackle this challenge, it is important to revisit the concept of an adjective: a word that describes such (e.g., smooth or rough); tells how many (e.g., two, few, many); or which one (e.g., this or that).

LANGUAGE FREQUENTLY CHANGES WITH EACH GENERATION. In the past, something good has been expressed as being bad, cool, gnarly, groovy, or awesome. Teenagers are often responsible for these word changes. Likewise, technology has slipped its specialized jargon into the mainstream. Because of Twitter, people can now "tweet." With the search engine Google, we can now be "Googled."

So what's the lowdown on this task's throw down? Select three common nouns, active verbs, or adjectives and change them into a different form to create a whole new meaning.

For example, take the word "numb." As an adjective, it describes a lack of sensation or feeling. As a verb, it is the action that causes the numb sensation, like when the dentist numbs your gum. But what about a *numb*? Using a little creativity, this word can now be used in a new way. Maybe it could mean the dull lead on your pencil. ("May I use the pencil sharpener? I've got a numb.")

On your paper, make three columns. Write the selected word in the first column, the new part of speech in the second, and in the third column write a short sentence that uses this word in its new form.

This task will take a little extra thinking. Are you "down" with that?

Ready? Take Five! 5!

odor-ific

To tackle this challenge, it is important to revisit the concept of an adjective: a word that describes (such as smooth or rough); tells how many (two, few); or which one (this or that).

AS YOU LEAVE THE BASKETBALL COURT, THE SMELL HITS YOU! You look around and spy a garbage can outside the gate. Slowly moving closer, you quickly confirm that is the source of the odor. Just how bad is it? On your W.A.L.L., describe the smell by making one extended comparison with another idea.

EXAMPLE

The smell was like the inside of my sneakers after running ten miles through two inches of mud and then leaving them in my closet for five days.

The smell was like a carton of milk that has been sitting on the counter for a week.

Now that's bad! Ready? Take Five!

LANGUAGE LINK

figurative language

LEARNING SETTING

individual

SUPPLIES
Student W.A.L.L.,

STANDARDS
Demonstrate understanding of figurative language, word relationships, and nuances in word meanings

Use precise words and phrases, relevant descriptive details, and sensory language to convey experiences and events

SUPPLIES

Student W.A.L.L.

Construction paper

Tape

Glue

Scissor

Skewer sticks

Desktop software program (opt.)

STANDARDS

Prepare for and participate effectively in a range of conversations and collaborations with diverse partners, building on others' ideas and expressing their own clearly and persuasively

Make strategic use of digital media (e.g., textual, graphic, audio, visual, and interactive elements) in presentations to enhance understanding of findings reasoning, and evidence and to add interest

TEACHER TIP:

How did the ancient Olympians prepare for their participation in the games? To take a virtual tour of this process, students can visit The British Museum's Ancient Greece webpage: **www. ancientgreece.co.uk**.

Here, students can follow day-to-day events of the Olympic Games by clicking on Games and Festivals.

olympic pride 1

ONE OF THE MOST MOVING MOMENTS of the Olympics is the parade of each country's athletes as they enter the stadium, proudly carrying their flag. Some flags have stars, crosses, and moons. Others simply have wide bands of color.

Unfortunately, you and your fellow teammates are the only athletes to represent your country, the teeny, tiny land of _____.

Using the materials provided, design and create your country's flag.

Ready? Take Five! **5!**

olympic pride 2

IN THE PREVIOUS TAKE FIVE, athletes were asked to create a flag to represent their country. In today's challenge, each team will present its flag, say the name of the country, and explain the event your team plans to enter—real or not!

Ready? Take Five! **5!**

LANGUAGE LINK
problem solving

LEARNING SETTING
collaboration

SUPPLIES

Student W.A.L.L.

Construction paper

Tape

Glue

Scissor

Skewer sticks

Desktop software program (opt.)

STANDARDS

Prepare for and participate effectively in a range of conversations and collaborations with diverse partners, building on others' ideas and expressing their own clearly and persuasively

Make strategic use of digital media (e.g., textual, graphic, audio, visual, and interactive elements) in presentations to enhance understanding of findings reasoning, and evidence and to add interest

TEACHER TIP

This activity can easily be extended over several days by allowing each game to be swapped from team to team. A manila envelope is necessary to contain each game. Additionally, a rating sheet could be included that allows teams to assess the game's instructions and fun factor!

SUPPLIES

Student W.A.L.L.

One sheet of plain paper

Toothpicks

A small piece of tape

Paper plate

Scissors

Markers (Items may be altered in any way)

STANDARDS

Analyze the main ideas and supporting details presented in diverse media and formats (e.g., visually, quantitatively, orally) and explain how the ideas clarify a topic, text, or issue under study

Use a variety of transition words, phrases, and clauses to convey sequence and signal shifts from one time frame or setting to another

olympic spirit

WHEN THE FIRST OLYMPIC GAMES WERE HELD in ancient Greece, events were few. Competition was limited to how fast an individual could run or perhaps throw a javelin or discus. Modern Olympics now include about 300 events from snowboarding to taekwondo and badminton.

Today's challenge is for each team to create a desktop Olympic event using only the materials provided. For instance, disks can be created from the paper or toothpicks broken and taped into a particular shape.

Divide team members so that some create the elements needed for the event while others write the directions.

At the completion, all events will need to be secured in folders or small paper bags so that the games can be pulled out and played another day.

Ready? Take Five!

one-eyed mystery

IN MYTHOLOGY, ODYSSEUS OUTSMARTED the powerful Cyclops (a giant with only one eye). What if we all had only one giant eye in the middle of our forehead? How would it change our daily lives?

Instead of considering what we could not do, what advantages can you "see" for having one eye? List four unusual ideas.

Ready? Take Five! **5!**

LANGUAGE LINK

cause-and-effect

LEARNING SETTING

individual

SUPPLIES
Student W.A.L.L.,

STANDARDS
Introduce a topic clearly, previewing what is to follow; organize ideas, concepts, and information, using strategies such as definition, classification, comparison/contrast, and cause/effect; include formatting (e.g., headings), graphics (e.g., charts, tables), and multimedia when useful to aiding comprehension

---

TEACHER TIP
Some examples might include saving money on contact lenses, having fewer distractions, and spending less time spent on applying eye makeup.

plot development

individual

SUPPLIES

Student W.A.L.L.

STANDARDS

Analyze how an author's choices concerning how to structure a text, order events within it (e.g., parallel plots), and manipulate time (e.g., pacing, flashback) create such effects as mystery, tension, or surprise that follows from the narrated experiences or events

Provide a conclusion

Write narratives to develop real or imagined experiences or events using effective technique, relevant descriptive details, and well-structured event sequences

overboard!

AGAINST THE INCOMING TIDE, Seth struggled to steer the small sailboat. Along for the Saturday afternoon ride, his friend Genny began to feel a bit concerned as she watched the dark clouds gather in the distance. The wind, just moments before a mere breeze, was now lashing at the sail.

Seeing a small island, Seth set his course in that direction. Just at that moment, however, a giant wave capsized the small craft, throwing them both into the sea. Struggling, they just managed to grab hold of the boat when another wave crashed overhead. Fear now gripped them both.

But then a miracle took place, making this a day they would never forget, an amazing tale to tell their future grandkids. What was this miracle? Explain by providing a resolution to their story in a descriptive paragraph.

Ready? Take Five!

panicked paddler

While tone is the author's attitude toward the subject, the mood, or atmosphere, reinforces the tone by events and descriptive details.

ALL IS QUIET ALONG THE RIVERBANKS. The lonely canoe slips through the shadows of the evening. The only sound is the quiet, rhythmic splash of the paddle as it cuts through the water. This drowsy mood is quickly cut short, however, when two reptilian eyes suddenly appear in the water ahead. The mood instantly becomes charged with anxiety as the paddler reacts to the sight of the alligator. As soon as he appears, however, the long reptile disappears beneath the murky water, and the canoe continues on its way.

Mood is all about the atmosphere that the writer chooses to create. Now that you are the writer, you will use the list of words provided to keep the mood changing as the paddler continues to encounter more adventures along his journey. Use at least three moods to continue the narrative above.

Moods: angry, lazy, desperate, eager, enthusiastic, romantic, intense, dark, disgusted, relieved.

Ready? Take Five!

LANGUAGE LINK

mood

LEARNING SETTING

individual

SUPPLIES
Student W.A.L.L.

STANDARDS
Use precise words and phrases, relevant descriptive details, and sensory language to convey experiences and events

Analyze how an author's choices concerning how to structure a text, order events within it (e.g., parallel plots), and manipulate time (e.g., pacing, flashback) create such effects as mystery, tension, or surprise

SUPPLIES
Student W.A.L.L.

STANDARDS
Develop the topic with relevant facts, definitions, concrete details, quotations, or other information and examples

Introduce claim(s) and organize the reasons and evidence clearly

TEACHER TIP
An assortment of plastic bags could accompany this challenge for visual prompting.

paper or plastic? 1

PAPER OR PLASTIC? UNLIKE OTHER MATERIALS, plastic doesn't disappear the moment it is tossed in the trash. It will sit in landfills for hundreds of years because it can't break down as easily as natural substances do, such as paper.

Plastic, however, is everywhere! It is in fabrics and pillows, cars, appliances, packaging, toothbrushes, fishing line, cell phones, shower curtains, and CDs. But what about all those plastic bags? List many unusual ways for plastic bags to be transformed and reused.

How about books made from recycled plastic bags so that pages won't get wet when a storm catches you by surprise?

Ready? Take Five!

paper or plastic? 2

PLASTIC DOESN'T SEEM TO BE GOING AWAY, at least not today! How would life be different if plastic had never been invented? For example, there wouldn't be AstroTurf for teams who play in covered stadiums or disposable silverware.

Without plastic, there would be more broken glass from bottles, meaning more cut fingers—and yet no Band-Aids to cover them. In fact, if you were to look around right now, you would see numerous items made of plastic: pencil sharpeners, pens, contact lenses, crates and shelving, clocks, table surfaces and chairs, computers, televisions . . . the list goes on and on.

Now it's your turn. Brainstorm to list the many ways life would be different without the invention of plastic.

Ready? Take Five!

LANGUAGE LINK
cause-and-effect

LEARNING SETTING
individual

SUPPLIES
Student W.A.L.L.

STANDARDS
Use words, phrases, and clauses to clarify the relationships among claim(s) and reasons

Develop the topic with relevant facts, definitions, concrete details, quotations, or other and examples

Introduce a topic clearly, previewing what is to follow; organize ideas, concepts, and information, using strategies such as definition, classification, comparison/contrast, and cause/effect; include formatting (e.g., headings), graphics (e.g., charts, tables), and multimedia when useful to aiding comprehension

TEACHER TIP
Students can also use the brainstorm and mind map functions on bubbl.us: **www. bubbl.us**.

SUPPLIES

Student W.A.L.L.

STANDARDS

Analyze how particular lines of dialogue or incidents in a story or drama propel the action, reveal aspects of a character, or provoke a decision

Draw evidence from literary or informational texts to support analysis reflection, and research

Introduce claim(s), acknowledge alternate or opposing claims, and organize the reasons and evidence logically

TEACHER TIP:

An interactive word search on peer pressure can be found at ProProfs' Brain Games: **www. proprofs.com/games/word -search/peer-pressure**. Those who successfully master the game will receive a certificate that can be shared on Facebook, Twitter, or MySpace.

Other interactive games can also be played here, such as puzzles and hangman word games, all dealing with social issues.

peer pressure

IN ARTHUR MILLER'S PLAY *THE CRUCIBLE*, a group of young girls create chaos in a small town when they accuse innocent victims of being witches.

One young girl is particularly taunted by the girls when she will not join them. No longer able to stand the pressure, she joins forces with them and begins to make her own false charges.

This situation may have been set in Salem, Massachusetts, during the 1600s, but the topic is still relevant today. Describe a time when you have felt pressured to do something you knew was wrong. How did you deal with the pressure? Would you handle it differently today? If so, how?

Ready? Take Five!

pencil magic

THE PENCIL IS A NECESSARY SCHOOL SUPPLY in the classroom. From this simple wooden tool stories emerge and poems take flight. The pencil, as an object, however, can have many other unusual uses. How about a mini rolling pin or a conductor's baton?

In this Take Five, you and your partner will brainstorm together, thinking of many different ways to use a pencil.

Place your answers into a cluster format by copying the graphic organizer below.

Ready? Take Five!

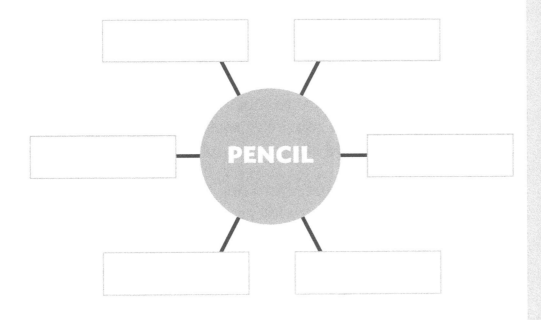

LANGUAGE LINK

graphic organizer

LEARNING SETTING

pair

SUPPLIES

Student W.A.L.L.

STANDARDS

Introduce a topic clearly, previewing what is to follow; organize ideas, concepts, and information, using strategies such as definition, classification, comparison/contrast, and cause/effect; include formatting (e.g., headings), graphics (e.g., charts, tables), and multimedia when useful to aiding comprehension

LANGUAGE LINK

sequencing

LEARNING SETTING

individual

SUPPLIES
Student W.A.L.L.

STANDARDS
Develop the topic with relevant facts, definition, concrete details, quotations, or other information and examples

Introduce a topic clearly, previewing what is to follow; organize ideas, concepts, and information, using strategies such as definition, classification, comparison/contrast, and cause/effect; include formatting (e.g., headings), graphics (e.g., charts, tables), and multimedia when useful to aiding comprehension

performing arts director

Among the many choices an author must make when writing is the order of details. This is known as sequencing, arranging details or actions in a particular order.

JUST IMAGINE IF ALL OF YOUR FAVORITE MUSICIANS were coming to your town for a special benefit concert. As director of the Performing Arts Center, you have a very difficult task–how to schedule the ten artists/groups who have agreed to perform.

To make the most money, you know you can't have the biggest acts first or you will lose revenue (money) from concession stand sales. All those soft drinks and tee shirts will go to waste if you don't keep the crowd's attention throughout the course of the evening.

To avoid this problem, you decide to schedule the musical acts from least important to most important, saving the top performer for last. First, make a list of all the performers you would like to schedule.

Next, number your paper from one to ten. Use your list to arrange the acts, starting with your least impressive and ending with number ten, your star headliner.

Ready? Take Five!

the pilgrims are coming

WHEN WILLIAM BRADFORD AND HIS FELLOW COMPANIONS set foot on Plymouth Rock, they found a strange new world. Fortunately for them, many lives were spared due to the help they received from Native Americans. The Native Americans shared their food with these colonists and taught them the skills needed for survival in the untamed wilderness.

Captain John Smith wrote in his journal about his encounter with the native population during his imprisonment. These journals and diaries detail the precarious beginnings of America's early immigrants.

But what about the other side of the story? For your challenge, you are to consider the arrival of these Europeans from the perspective of the Native Americans. Your diary entry may tell a different story. Record your own thoughts, insight, and predictions in a diary entry format.

Ready? Take Five!

LANGUAGE LINK
point of view

LEARNING SETTING
individual

SUPPLIES
Student W.A.L.L.

STANDARDS
Assess how point of view or purpose shapes the content and style of a text

Use narrative techniques, such as dialogue, pacing, description, and reflection, to develop experiences, events, and/or characters

TEACHER TIP
Excellent articles and videos on the first Thanksgiving can be found at History.com (**www.history.com/topics/plymouth**).

LANGUAGE LINK

descriptive writing

LEARNING SETTING

individual

SUPPLIES

Student W.A.L.L.

Thesaurus

STANDARDS

Use precise words and phrases, relevant descriptive details, and sensory language to convey experiences and events

Consult reference materials (e.g., dictionaries, glossaries, thesauruses), both print and digital, to find the pronunciation of a word or determine or clarify its precise meaning or its part of speech

TEACHER TIP

Students will enjoy creating their own pirate story using Kerpoof Studio's "Tell a Story" tool (**www.kerpoof.com/#/activity/ storybook**).

pirates

IN THE DISTANCE, YOU AND YOUR CREWMATES have spotted the Jolly Roger, the crossbones flag of a motley pirate crew. Today will not be the day to outrun them, however. Their ship is too powerful and fast. Fear ripples through all on board.

All too soon, the enemy is upon you. Their cannons and guns are lined up and ready should resistance be spotted. All is quiet as they lower their ropes and drop aboard— but what a surprise awaits you all! Unlike the stereotype of pirates with bandanas, beards, and eye patches, these are quite different. Though they are just as terrifying, it is in a very weird way.

Your task is to describe two of these individuals using very descriptive language. Provide a name for each individual. Beneath the name, create a list of very vivid descriptions.

For example, there's Black Jack: completely red – his skin and clothing; sharp lobster claws for hands; a bushy mustache so long he braids each end and ties it together atop his head.

A thesaurus may be used for this task.

Ready, matey? Take Five!

play ball 1

GOLF, HOCKEY, LACROSSE, BASEBALL . . . these games have one thing in common. They all use a ball and a stick, a set of rules, and a marked playing field. In this task, your team will create a game using the materials provided.

The first challenge will involve planning a game that will use a miniature ball and playing stick (paper wad and straw). Decide the objective of the game and the rules for play. Write these on the note card. Simplicity works best.

Ready? Take Five! 5!

LANGUAGE LINK

sequencing

LEARNING SETTING

collaboration

SUPPLIES (PER TEAM):

2 drinking straws

2 paper cups

2 popsicle sticks

2 sheets of paper

Note card

Pencil

Tape

Two paperclips

STANDARDS

Use a variety of transition words, phrases, and clauses to convey sequence and signal shifts from one time frame or setting to another

TEACHER TIP

Three days need to be allotted for this sequential prompt.

LANGUAGE LINK

sequencing

LEARNING SETTING

collaboration

SUPPLIES (PER TEAM):

2 drinking straws

2 paper cups

2 popsicle sticks

2 sheets of paper

2 paperclips

Note card

Pencil

Tape

STANDARDS

Use a variety of transition words, phrases, and clauses to convey sequence and signal shifts from one time frame or setting to another

play ball 2

THIS NEXT TASK IS TO DRAW THE PLAYING FIELD and any special penalty boxes, gridlines, or other features. Some members of the group might want to spend time refining the rules from the previous day. Be sure to secure the items for this task in the manila envelope and label it with your game's name.

Ready? Take Five!

play ball 3

IT'S DAY THREE AND PLAYERS ARE READY to take to the field! It's been a long process, but now you have a game that you can pull out and play at a later time, exchanging with other teams to test their ability to accurately provide directions in a clearly written sequence.

Ready? Take Five!

SUPPLIES (PER TEAM):

2 drinking straws

2 paper cups

2 popsicle sticks

2 sheets of paper

Note card

Pencil

Tape

Two paperclips

STANDARDS

Use a variety of transition words, phrases, and clauses to convey sequence and signal shifts from one time frame or setting to another

LANGUAGE LINK
mood

LEARNING SETTING
individual

SUPPLIES
Student W.A.L.L.

STANDARDS
Determine the meaning of words and phrases as they are used in a text, including figurative and connotative meanings; analyze the impact of a specific word choice on meaning and tone

Use precise words and phrases, telling details, and sensory language to convey a vivid picture of the experiences, events, setting, and/or characters

TEACHER TIP
More information on Poe and his works can be found at PoeStories .com (**www.poestories.com**).

In addition, students can discover an interactive version of "The Raven" that highlights literary devices used in the poem with a quick swipe of the cursor over color-coded text. This can be found at TeachersFirst's "Interactive Raven": **http:// legacy.teachersfirst.com/share/ raven/start-fl.html**.

poetic madness

AMERICAN WRITER EDGAR ALLAN POE IS A MASTER of spooky stories that often include murder and madness. Each detail is carefully crafted to reflect the mood he wants to develop; details like a long crack in an old family mansion, a dungeon filled with skeletons, a screeching cat, or a dreary day in December.

Currently, Poe is feeling a little under the weather. His creative juices just aren't flowing like they normally do. What he can't seem to pull out are those amazing details. While he takes a vacation from Boston for a short vacation in the Bahamas, he needs your help.

Create five details that would reflect this creepy mood—details that could fit easily into any Poe short story or poem. What about a dark, musty attic where rats can be heard scurrying about? You definitely wouldn't want to be there!

When he returns, Poe will be using these in his story. Aim for very descriptive, vivid images.

Ready? Take Five!

popsicle sentences

A quick review on these parts of speech might help for this prompt. ***Noun****s can be persons, places, things, or ideas (e.g., sister, Nevada, chain, hope).* ***Adjectives*** *are words that describe or tell how many (e.g., lovely, tiny, one), while* ***adverbs*** *tell how or when something is done (e.g., slowly, now, often).* ***Verbs*** *express action or a state of being (e.g., is, jump, seem, crack).*

ALL MIXED UP! THAT IS WHAT HAPPENS when words come tumbling from a bag. Each group of four students, however, will bring order to the whole mess. In front of each group are eight bags. In each bag are two popsicle sticks. Two bags are labeled nouns and two bags are labeled descriptive adjectives while the others are labeled active verbs and adverbs.

Quickly distribute two bags to each person in the group in any order. Using markers, write two different words that correspond to the bag's label. If it is labeled "noun," write a different noun on each popsicle stick (e.g., whale and beehive). They may be proper or common nouns. After all the sticks are labeled, prepare for the sixty-second sentence maker.

At the signal, toss all sticks on the table and construct the longest sentence using all the words. Articles (a, an, the) are free and may be used at any time. Set the bags aside and save them for another Take Five moment (swapping bags among different groups).

EXAMPLE

The cow suddenly crashed into a shy tree.

Ready? Take Five! 5!

SUPPLIES

Popsicle sticks

Paper bags

Markers

STANDARDS

Demonstrate command of the conventions of standard English grammar and usage when writing or speaking

Acknowledge new information expressed by others and, when warranted, modify their own views

TEACHER TIP

Tuck these bags of word games aside for use on another day. As knowledge of sentence-building increases, other components can be added (e.g., coordinate conjunctions, prepositions).

Arcademic Skill Builders provides a fun way to interactively review parts of speech through a "Word Invasion" game: **www. arcademicskillbuilders.com/ games/invasion/invasion .html**

LANGUAGE LINK

cause-and-effect

LEARNING SETTING

individual

SUPPLIES

Student W.A.L.L.

STANDARDS

Provide a conclusion that follows from and reflects on what is experienced, observed, or resolved over the course of the narrative

Introduce a topic clearly, previewing what is to follow; organize ideas, concepts, and information, using strategies such as definition, classification, comparison/contrast, and cause/effect; include formatting (e.g., headings), graphics (e.g., charts, tables), and multimedia when useful to aiding comprehension

pot of gold

THE LEPRECHAUN OF ALLENWOOD has served as guardian of the legendary pot of gold for many years. Each morning finds him standing guard at the end of the rainbow . . . until today. A terrible cold has kept him in bed. Instead, he has persuaded his cousin, the Leprechaun of Crookhaven, to take his place for the day.

Now, the Leprechaun of Crookhaven isn't as honest as his cousin. Maybe the Leprechaun of Allenwood knew this, because when his greedy cousin actually lifted the lid to peer into the pot, it wasn't gold he found.

In a well-developed paragraph, describe what is in the pot and what happens as Leprechaun of Crookhaven frantically tries to fit the stubborn lid back into place once again.

Ready? Take Five!

punctuation art

THE POET e.e. cummings (as he preferred to write his name) rarely used them—punctuation marks. These innocent dots, dashes, and curves tell readers when to take a break, when to keep things moving, when to add information, and when to omit something. In this task, however, you will be elevating their common status to an original work of art.

SELECT ONE OF THE FOLLOWING MARKS OF PUNCTUATION:

comma	,	question mark	?
period	.	exclamation mark	!
semicolon	;	parentheses	()
colon	:	quotation mark	" "
apostrophe	'	bracket	[]
ellipses	. . .	hyphen	-

In bold color, place your punctuation mark on the paper. Be sure to make it large enough and bold enough so that it can be recognized as the centerpiece for your work of art. Make use of lighter or pastel shades to add the rest of the details in this original work of art so that the punctuation mark remains clearly visible.

It can be realistic (a picture of something specific and recognizable) or abstract (a piece that depicts a mood without specific, identifiable features).

Ready? Take Five! 5!

LANGUAGE LINK
punctuation

LEARNING SETTING
individual

SUPPLIES
Plain and construction paper

Markers/Colored pencils

STANDARDS
Demonstrate command of the conventions of standard English capitalization, punctuation, and spelling when writing or speaking

Interpret information presented in diverse media and formats (e.g., visually, quantitatively, orally) and explain how it contributes to a topic, text, or issue under study

TEACHER TIP
Although this prompt begins with one mark of punctuation, more visual representations can be added with the addition of extra marks of punctuation in each work of art.

LANGUAGE LINK
punctuation

LEARNING SETTING
individual[5]

SUPPLIES
Student W.A.L.L.

STANDARDS
Demonstrate command of the conventions of standard English capitalization, punctuation, and spelling when writing

punctuation woes

*A quick review of the types of sentences is needed for this prompt. An **interrogative sentence** asks a questions and end with a question mark. An **exclamatory sentence** expresses surprise or strong feeling. It ends with an exclamation mark. An **imperative sentence** is one that gives a command, direction, or request. It ends with a period and begins with the understood subject: you. A **declarative sentence** is a sentence that makes a statement. It ends with a period.*

UH, OH! ANGIE HAS A WILD STORY TO TELL THE POLICE officer who just pulled her over for speeding. In this task, you will complete the conversation between Angie and the police officer.

But there's a catch! You must use the same sequence of punctuation marks and sentence types after each line: a question (interrogative), an exclamation mark (exclamatory), a period (imperative) and then a period in a final declarative sentence.

Confused? Read the following conversation carefully and watch how the sequence of sentence types is used.

> Officer: "Do you know why I pulled you over?" (Interrogative)
> Angie: "But officer!" (Exclamatory)
> Officer: "Don't try to give me any excuses." (Imperative)
> Angie: "I'm really sorry, but I think I need to tell you what just happened." (Declarative)

Now it's your turn to continue Angie's tale of woe. Create four more sentences in the exact order of the model: interrogative, exclamatory, imperative, declarative.

Ready? Take Five! 5!

quote me

UNABLE TO CONTAIN HER ENTHUSIASM, HALEY SHOT DOWN the hallway to her first class of the day, waving a letter in her tightly clenched hand. She couldn't wait to share her news with her friends. T.K. and all her other classmates were just beginning to settle into their seats when she abruptly stopped in the open doorway and shouted . . . what?

What news could be that exciting? Using quotation marks, provide at least three different answers to that question.

Ready? Take Five!

LANGUAGE LINK

punctuation

LEARNING SETTING

individual

SUPPLIES
Student W.A.L.L.

STANDARDS
Demonstrate command of the conventions of standard English capitalization, punctuation, and spelling when writing

Use narrative technique such as dialogue, pacing, and description to develop experiences, events, and/or characters

LANGUAGE LINK

main idea

LEARNING SETTING

individual

SUPPLIES

Markers

Newsprint strips or other plain paper strips

Desktop publishing software (opt.)

STANDARDS

Determine a theme or central ideas of a text and how it is conveyed through particular details; provide a summary of the text distinct from personal opinions of judgments

Analyze how a particular sentence, chapter, scene, or stanza fits into the overall structure of a text and contributes to the development of the theme, setting, or plot

TEACHER TIP

After completing this challenge, sample headlines can be displayed around the media center to help spur interest in reading class favorites.

read all about it

READ ALL ABOUT IT! "Abused juvenile delinquent discovers treasure in hole." If the plot developed in the book *Holes* by Louis Sachar were truth instead of fiction, this might be the morning news headline.

Consider this example using *Tears of a Tiger*: "student killed in accident, friends try to cope." Consider the possibilities with other books or short stories you have read.

This activity is to take the plot of two different books or short stories and turn them into headlines. Use the strips of newsprint or your computer to write your headlines.

Ready? Take Five!

recipe for failure

LANGUAGE LINK
editing

LEARNING SETTING
individual[5]

SUPPLIES
Student W.A.L.L.

STANDARDS
Demonstrate command of the conventions of standard English grammar and usage when writing or speaking

Demonstrate command of the conventions of standard English capitalization, punctuation, and spelling when writing

Develop and strengthen writing as needed by planning, revising, editing, rewriting, or trying a new approach, focusing on addressing what is most significant for a specific purpose and audience

WHEN IT COMES TO WRITING A PAPER, most students know the basic rules for getting there: correct punctuation, focus on a specific topic, well-developed supporting details, good grammar, and accurate spelling. Just as important, however, is to know what it takes to receive an F on a paper!

This can be just as revealing–and sometimes just as helpful. These are the things you don't want to do! Place yourself in the role of the teacher. Plowing through a tall stack of papers, he has just reached your essay. His red pen stands ready to do some serious damage. He begins reading and a scowl appears upon his face as the pen takes its first swipe, followed by another and then another. As he finally lays the essay to rest, it bleeds with red markings from introduction to conclusion. What criminal sins of the writing world have you committed?

THE F NOW ENGRAVED IN THE MARGIN OF YOUR ESSAY reflects five major errors you have committed. List these errors on one side of your paper. Beside each error, explain how you could avoid this problem in the future.

EXAMPLE

Common errors	*How errors can be avoided*
Going off topic in an essay statement	*Be sure all supporting details and examples reflect the thesis*

Ready? Take Five!

graphic organizer

individual

SUPPLIES
Student W.A.L.L.

STANDARDS
Introduce a topic clearly, previewing what is to follow; organize ideas, concepts, and information, using strategies such as definition, classification, comparison/contrast, and cause/effect; include formatting (e.g., headings), graphics (e.g., charts, tables), and multimedia when useful to aiding comprehension

Use words, phrases, and clauses to create cohesion and clarify the relationships among claim(s), reasons, and evidence

---

TEACHER TIP
Once students have exhausted their own ideas, they can get help from the Museum of Fine Arts, Houston's "Historical/Cultural Timeline" at **www.fm.coe .uh .edu/timeline/1600s.html**.

return of robinson crusoe

THE DATE IS JUNE 11, 1687. You are the first reporter on the scene when Robinson Crusoe returns to England after being stranded on an island for 28 years. During the interview, you learn that living on an island has its drawbacks and its advantages.

To assist you in taking notes, make a two-column graphic organizer with "disadvantages" at the top of one column and "advantages" at the top of the second column. What did you discover during your interview?

EXAMPLE

Disadvantages	*Advantages*
"No Sunday morning newspaper"	*"Island champ in Tic-Tac-Toe"*

Ready? Take Five!

rock, paper, scissors

MANY CHILDREN LEARN TO SETTLE DIFFERENCES with the simple game of "rock, paper, scissors." In this traditional game, players pump closed fists three times; the third time, however, players select to keep a closed fist (rock), extend two fingers (for scissors), or create a flat surface (paper).

The winner is decided in the following order of strength: rock crushes scissors; paper covers rock; scissors cut paper. Who gets the last piece of cake? Rock, paper, scissors. Who has to take out the trash? Rock, paper, scissors. The game originated from its Japanese ancestor called "Jan Ken Pon."

In this task, you and your partner will be playing against each other as you develop a newer version of this game. An example might go something like this in the game of "Turtle, Rabbit, Skunk":

Representations and Strength

Turtle: (closed fist with two fingers wrapped over the thumb to represent the shell).
Turtle beats skunk.

Rabbit: (fist with second and third fingers pointed up for rabbit ears).
Rabbit beats turtle.

Skunk: (a closed fist with pinkie finger extended for the raised tail).
Skunk beats rabbit.

Develop your own characters, their representations, and their order of power. Keep your rules handy as you play! Deep thinking and concentration are needed for this game.

Ready? Take Five! 5!

SUPPLIES
Student W.A.L.L.

STANDARDS
Follow rules for collegial discussions and decision-making, track progress toward specific goals and deadlines, and define individual roles as needed

Use words, phrases, and clauses to create cohesion and clarify the relationships among claim(s), reasons, and evidence

LANGUAGE LINK

characterization

LEARNING SETTING

individual[5]

SUPPLIES
Student W.A.L.L.

STANDARDS
Analyze how and why individuals, events, and ideas develop and interact over the course of a text

Use narrative techniques, such as dialogue, pacing, and description, to develop experiences, events, and/or characters

TEACHER TIP
Students will have fun listing a variety of questions that could be asked of Romeo and Juliet. For a humorous extension, students could exchange questions with one another and then provide their own unique answers.

romeo, romeo 1

SHAKESPEARE'S ROMEO AND JULIET IS A TRAGIC PLAY about two love-struck teenagers who can't be together because their families are feuding—not getting along at all! Forced to meet in secret, they soon pledge their love to each other.

Before things can get too out of hand, however, Friar Laurence thinks they should both go to counseling. You are the psychiatrist. With Romeo now at ease on the couch, psychoanalyze this young man from Verona, Italy.

What questions could you ask as you attempt to analyze him? List three in-depth questions you might ask of him. Next on the couch is fair Juliet. What three questions would you ask of her?

EXAMPLES

To Juliet

"So do you feel there is a relationship problem between you and your father?"

To Romeo

"Were you picked on as a child?"

Ready? Take Five!

romeo, romeo 2

NOW THAT YOU HAVE ANALYZED ROMEO AND JULIET in a previous Take Five, select any other fictional character who might need your professional help.

Provide a description of this person (or thing), and then create at least three questions for your patient.

Ready? Take Five!

LANGUAGE LINK

characterization

LEARNING SETTING

individual

SUPPLIES

Student W.A.L.L.

STANDARDS

Analyze how and why individuals, events, and ideas develop and interact over the course of a text

Use narrative techniques, such as dialogue, pacing, and description, to develop experiences, events, and/or characters

TEACHER TIP

This activity provides an excellent follow up to a novel or short story study.

persuasive writing

individual

SUPPLIES

Student W.A.L.L.

STANDARDS

Write arguments to support claims in an analysis of substantive topics or texts, using valid reasoning and relevant and sufficient evidence

save the zoo

OH NO! THE BUDGET CRUNCH IS ABOUT TO HIT the local zoo. There just isn't enough money to keep the zoo open for another year. When it closes, all animals will be sent to new homes in zoos all across the country. This just can't happen!

Your task is to design a unique way to raise money for the zoo. Caution: You must think big–as big as the elephants that live in your zoo. Also, the plan must be linked in some way to the animals. For example, you could auction off each animal to local businesses and organizations— not literally, of course. Highest bidders would win the opportunity to have their name, business, or logo attached to that animal's exhibit.

Now it's your turn. Create a plan to raise money for the zoo. Next, write a convincing argument addressed to the Board of Directors.

Ready? Take Five!

say hey, kids!

WALK DOWN ANY GREETING CARD AISLE and you will find miles of displays with a card for almost any situation–birthdays, anniversaries, retirement, moving away, a promotion, even "I'm sorry."

Today, Hallmark Cards needs your help. The company wants to design a series of cards devoted to the thirteen and under crowd. They want cards that will express new and different ideas: "Just wait 'til next year" (a card for fellow teammates); "Encore! Encore!" (a card for someone who has been in a play or performed in a concert).

What might be some topics of concern to this age group? What about a card with an anti-bullying message or a "You're the Best" card—one that lets recipients know how much you appreciate them?

Fold a half sheet of paper in half or open a new word processing document. This is your blank card. Next, create a prototype, or model, for a card that would be popular with your audience.

Ready? Take Five!

LANGUAGE LINK

creative writing

LEARNING SETTING

individual

SUPPLIES

Student W.A.L.L.

Half sheet of plain paper

Markers

Desktop design software (opt.)

STANDARDS

Analyze the structure of texts, including how specific sentences, paragraphs, and larger portions of the text (e.g., a section, chapter, scene, or stanza) relate to each other and the whole

Develop the topic with relevant facts, definitions, concrete details, quotations, or other information and examples

Make strategic use of digital media (e.g., textual, graphical, audio, visual, and interactive elements) in presentations to enhance understanding of findings, reasoning, and evidence and to add interest

SUPPLIES

Strips of construction paper or newsprint

Markers

STANDARDS

Develop the topic with relevant facts, definitions, concrete details, quotations, or other information and examples

TEACHER TIP

If you don't have a copy of Benjamin Franklin's Poor Richard's Almanack, a work filled with many aphorisms coined by Franklin, then visit PoorRichards. net (**www.poorrichards.net/ benjamin-franklin**) to share more of Franklin's popular aphorisms with students.

say what?

Unlike slang or clichés, aphorisms are short statements that express truths that are not limited by time or place.

ACCORDING TO BENJAMIN FRANKLIN, "A penny saved is a penny earned," and likewise, "Eat to live and not live to eat." A more modern writer, James Geary, once stated that "Laughter blows away the dust from our eyes," and "People lose common sense when they gain dollars and cents."

Short phrases that express a popular truth are called aphorisms. Today you will create your own unique saying and use the markers provided to write your aphorism on a strip of construction paper.

Feel free to decorate.

Ready? Take Five!

scavenger hunt

IT'S TIME FOR A SCAVENGER HUNT! In groups of three to four, use notebooks, book bags, or purses to discover a list of items in the five-minute time limit.

Though textbooks may be used for obtaining items, they cannot be presented in the final tally. Items from a textbook must be copied on paper and submitted with the other objects found in this challenge.

This challenge is to be tackled without the use of computers. This is where teamwork and delegation of jobs really counts! Which team will find the most items? Items are as follows:

a penny from 1995 or earlier

a picture of a cartoon character

an identification card

a pencil with a slogan

the name of a British writer

a synonym for "emaciated"

the definition of the word "sonnet"

a picture of a place

Ready? Take Five! **5!**

LANGUAGE LINK
problem solving

LEARNING SETTING
collaboration

STANDARDS
Consult reference materials (e.g., dictionaries, glossaries, thesauruses), both print and digital, to find the pronunciation of a word or determine or clarify its precise meaning or its part of speech

Follow rules for collegial discussions, set specific goals and deadlines, and define individual roles as needed

TEACHER TIP
Many online scavenger hunts allow students additional learning opportunities. For example, the Adventures of CyberBee website sends students on a search for information about contemporary writers such as Avi and R.L. Stine: **www.cyberbee.com/author _sites.htm**.

SUPPLIES

Plain paper

Colored pencils

Software paint tool (opt.)

STANDARDS

Make strategic use of digital media and visual displays of data to express information and enhance understanding of presentations

Integrate and evaluate information presented in diverse media and formats, including visually, quantitatively, and orally

Develop the topic with relevant facts, definitions, concrete details, quotations, or other information and examples

TEACHER TIP

Logos can be strategically displayed around the school. For an added bonus to this activity, students can select the one they feel best represents their school. The logo can then be taken from draft to final stage in representing the school in visual form on the school website.

school logo

LOOK AROUND, AND YOU ARE ALMOST CERTAIN TO SEE one—a logo. Logos readily identify a product or a corporation. Some popular logos include Nike's "swoosh," McDonald's golden arches, NBC's peacock, and Klondike's polar bear.

Along with the logo image, the typography of the brand name itself is very important. Nintendo uses easy-to-read letters while Coca Cola creates interest with its swirls of red or white script.

Now it's time for you and a partner to create a logo for your school. Consider factors such as the following: the location of your school (river, mountains, or desert), any unique characteristics it may have, and the mission statement of the school.

Think beyond the school's mascot. Use the paper and colored pencils to create your design or use the paint tool on your computer. Below the logo, provide a brief explanation of how the logo reflects your school. Think positive!

Ready? Take Five!

school supplies

THE SUMMER IS BARELY HALF OVER, and already stores are beginning their annual back-to-school sales. Racks of boardshorts for guys and tees for girls are being replaced with khaki shorts, collared shirts, and backpacks. Long aisles near the front of the store are being stocked with binders and notebook paper, pencils, and dividers.

Up and down each aisle, tired parents steer their carts while tightly clutching their child's school supply list. Following far behind are the students themselves, who stop along the way to admire fluorescent pencil sharpeners and neon-colored note cards.

Some of the most important items on that back-to-school list never appear, however. What if your list began in this manner?

1. Never allow a bully to control your life.
2. If you see a new student, invite her or him to eat lunch with you and your friends.
3. Pack extra pencils for classmates whose parents may not be able to take them back-to-school shopping.

Now it's your turn. From your experiences, what would your back-to-school list be? Make a list of five "items."

Ready? Take Five!

LANGUAGE LINK

expository writing

LEARNING SETTING

individual

SUPPLIES
Student W.A.L.L.

STANDARDS
Introduce a topic: organize ideas, concepts, and information, using strategies such as definition, classification, comparison/contrast, and cause/effect; include formatting (e.g., headings), graphic (e.g., charts, tables), and multimedia when useful to aiding comprehension

persuasive writing

individual[5]

SUPPLIES
Student W.A.L.L.

STANDARDS

Write arguments to support claims in an analysis of substantive topics or texts, using valid reasoning and relevant and sufficient evidence

Demonstrate command of the conventions of standard English grammar and usage when writing or speaking

TEACHER TIP
Despite the ease of quick and easy e-mails, letter writing still has a place in today's world. This activity can easily be extended to incorporate formal letter-writing basics.

schoolhouse rock

THINGS ARE PRETTY ROCKY AT THE LOCAL SCHOOL BOARD! Much to some students' dismay, more and more school systems are turning to longer school years to help increase standardized test scores. Your local school board is willing to try anything to increase student performance.

In the next few hours, they will be voting on extending the school year by an additional three weeks! Many people are on the agenda to speak in support of–or against–this measure. Your name is on the list.

Develop your most persuasive argument with specific details to support your position. It's now your turn. "Dear honorable school board members . . ." you begin. On your paper, write your argument.

Ready? Take Five! **5!**

secret cipher 1

VICTORIA, YOUR LITTLE SISTER, LOVES TO PRY in your room. Nothing escapes her, particularly notes from your friends. Fortunately, you have an idea. You and your friends have decided to use a code.

This is what your sister will read tonight: "Can Amy loan Lynn my emerald turkey? Odd Nelly insists Gina have Todd ask Trena Smith in Xodelphia." By taking the first letter of each word the actual message is revealed: "Call me tonight at six."

Another message is needed. What will Victoria read tomorrow night, and what will the actual message be?

Ready? Take Five!

LANGUAGE LINK
problem solving

LEARNING SETTING
individual

SUPPLIES
Student W.A.L.L.

STANDARDS
Read closely to determine what the text says explicitly and to make logical inferences from it; cite specific textual evidence when writing or speaking to support conclusions drawn from the text

TEACHER TIP
The difference between a code and a cipher is that a code substitutes symbols for letters and words while a cipher uses letters in different combinations to form words and phrases. More informational reading, along with examples of codes and ciphers, can be found at The Museum of Unnatural Mystery website: **www.unmuseum.org/cipher .htm**.

problem solving

pair

SUPPLIES

Student W.A.L.L.

STANDARDS

Read closely to determine what the text says explicitly and to make logical inferences from it; cite specific textual evidence when writing or speaking to support conclusions drawn from the text

secret cipher 2

IN THIS CHALLENGE, ANOTHER CIPHER IS NEEDED. Today, you will develop your own cipher using any arrangement of letters. Write a short message and then switch with a partner to decipher, or break, each cipher!

For instance, if you write a message backwards without using any punctuation, you would read: "Niagagnipoonssiairotciv" (Victoria is snooping again.) This prompt "stset" students' cipher-breaking skills.

Ready? Take Five!

secret messages

THROUGHOUT HISTORY, SECRET MESSAGES have been written and sent using codes and ciphers. Often, a symbol or number would be used in place of words or a letter of the alphabet. The German army thought it had the most unbreakable of all codes—until it was broken, and their military plans were revealed. Early civilizations used torches or smoke to send their secret messages.

For the beginning cryptographer (a person who makes, breaks, and sends messages using codes), the simplest way to create a secret message is by substituting a number for a letter of the alphabet. The number one, for example, could represent the letter A. If your name were Alex, the code for your name would be a 1 12 5 24.

What would your name be if written in this code? Use the same idea to write your own secret message and pass it to a partner to break.

Ready? Take Five! **5!**

LANGUAGE LINK
problem solving

LEARNING SETTING
pair

SUPPLIES
Student W.A.L.L.

STANDARDS
Use the relationship between particular words (e.g., cause/effect, part/whole, item category) to better understand each of the words

Cite textual evidence to support analysis of what the text says explicitly as well as inferences drawn from the text

TEACHER TIP
Students can discover the stories of the Navajo Code Talkers at their official website (**www.navajocodetalkers.org**) and hear these veterans of World War II describe their role in the war effort.

Students can test their own code-breaking skills by playing the CIA's "Break the Code" game at **https://www.cia.gov/kids-page/games/break-the-code**.

LANGUAGE LINK
sequencing

LEARNING SETTING
individual

SUPPLIES
Note cards

STANDARDS
Use appropriate transitions to clarify the relationships among ideas and concepts

Use precise language and domain-specific vocabulary to manage the complexity of the topic

TEACHER TIP

A delicious extension of this prompt would test students' ability to follow directions—or possibly their writing skills— by having students bring their ingredients to class and then having someone else read the card and attempt to follow the directions.

Examples of transitions could include the following: Next, then, after that, following this, before, and at this point.

For more information on transitional words and phrases, visit the "Transitional Devices" page of the Purdue Online Writing Lab website: **http://owl.english.purdue.edu/owl/resource/574/02**

secret recipe

NO ONE MAKES _____ QUITE LIKE YOU DO. According to your closest friends, it is the best dessert ever! Best of all, no baking is necessary. Everyone wants the recipe, but you have kept it a close secret—until now.

At the top of your note card, write the name of the dessert. Beneath that, list all the ingredients (no more than five), and then explain the steps needed to create this wonderful treat.

For example, what about Chocolate Banana Freeze made with crushed banana popsicles, chocolate pudding, and whipped cream? Be sure the instructions are easy to follow in a step-by-step manner and that transitional words and phrases are used to help the reader move from one sequence to the next.

Ready? Take Five!

sequel

TWO SIMPLE WORDS CAN STRIKE FEAR INTO THE HEART and soul of an engaged reader: "The End." Many books leave the reader wanting more. Sequels help satisfy that need. How would you treat a favorite novel if you could write the sequel?

In this task, you are to select one of your favorite books that doesn't have a sequel. Some possibilities for sequel status might be found in the following list: *Charlotte's Web, Tuck Everlasting, Lord of the Flies, The Witch of Blackbird Pond, The Call of the Wild, Freaky Friday, Frankenstein*, and *Squashed*.

Once you have made your selection, create your own adventure. Provide a summary and a title for this book.

Ready? Take Five!

LANGUAGE LINK

summary

LEARNING SETTING

individual

SUPPLIES
Student W.A.L.L.

STANDARDS
Write narratives to develop real or imagined experiences or events using effective technique, well-chosen details, and well-structured event sequences

Determine central ideas or themes of a text and analyze their development; summarize the key supporting details and ideas

Assess how point of view or purpose shapes the content and style of a text

LANGUAGE LINK
cause-and-effect

LEARNING SETTING
individual

SUPPLIES
Student W.A.L.L.

STANDARDS
Introduce claim(s) and organize the reasons and evidence clearly

Introduce a topic; organize ideas, concepts, and information, using strategies such as definition, classification, comparison/ contrast, and cause/effect; include formatting (e.g., headings), graphic (e.g., charts, tables), and multimedia when useful to aiding comprehension

Develop the topic with relevant facts, definitions, concrete details, quotations, or other information and examples

TEACHER TIP
This prompt can be extended for another day's use (e.g., if humans had rubber for skin, if humans could change colors like a chameleon, if humans were covered with suction cups).

slithery, slimy, scaly

FISH, DINOSAURS, AND EVEN SNAKES HAVE THEM—SCALES. Consider what life would be like if humans had scales all over their bodies. Copy the graphic organizer below and record your unique responses in each circle.

Creative ideas can be stretched as far as your imagination will take them in this prompt. Black vinyl scales that move back and forth can be your own personal fan on a hot day!

Scales can be any size, shape, material, or color. The scales can be a positive asset, or they can be a huge burden for daily activities.

Ready? Take Five! 5!

if humans had scales

S.O.S.

MORSE CODE ALLOWS TEXT, OR PRINTED WORDS, to be translated into a series of dots and dashes so that listeners can copy the sounds they hear and then translate the message. s.o.s. is the international Morse code distress signal. Movies frequently show worried sailors typing out the traditional ...------... (s.o.s.) code when their ship is in danger of sinking.

What if you had your own distress call, one to use when you feel you are losing an important game or failing a test?

Suppose you were in the middle of a spelling bee and halfway through the word your mind goes blank. What if you could send a distress call and help would immediately come your way? Your task is to develop your own unique s.o.s.

Your code can be letters, words, motions, or sounds. Explain what the signal is, what happens when it's sent, and examples of circumstances when it could be used.

In the case of the spelling bee, your distress call (a tap on the nose) gave you an extra five minutes, giving you the chance to regroup and relax before tackling the task again.

Ready? Take Five! 5!

LANGUAGE LINK

expository writing

LEARNING SETTING

individual

SUPPLIES
Student W.A.L.L.

Half sheet of plain paper

Markers

STANDARDS
Write informative/explanatory texts to examine a topic and convey ideas, concepts, and information through the selection, organization, and analysis of relevant content

Determine the meaning of words and phrases as they are used in a text, including figurative, connotative, and technical meanings

TEACHER TIP
Students can experiment with typing their own names, phrases, or sentences into a Morse Code Translator on the Qbit website (**www.qbit.it/lab/morse.php**).

Here, they will not only be able to see the code, but hear it as well.

figurative language

individual

SUPPLIES

Student W.A.L.L.

STANDARDS

Demonstrate understanding of figurative language, word relationships, and nuances in word meanings

Develop the topic with relevant facts, definitions, concrete details, quotations, or other information and examples

TEACHER TIP

The interactive "Exploring Onomatopoeia" page of ReadWriteThink allows students to stretch their descriptive vocabulary as they listen to six different sounds and then type their responses in the boxes provided: **http://nteractives.mped.org/preview_mg.aspx?id=736**.

sounds like sizzz

When bees buzz and storms rumble, they are prime candidates for writers who want to steal their thunder—literally. Onomatopoeia is a literary device that takes sounds and turns them into words.

DROWSILY, YOU AWAKE TO THE SOUND OF THE ALARM— "buzz!" Slowly, you make your way into the bathroom and turn on the faucet—"keuuu" comes the stream of water. In the kitchen, bacon is frying—"sizzz"—and ice cubes drop into your glass—"ka-plop."

Now begins the rest of your day, onomatopoeia style. Describe the rest of your day, not in words but in sounds. No explanations are needed, just a long list of sounds until you head to bed.

Ready? Take Five!

speak, fido!

The key to using quotation marks is knowing how to pair them with punctuation marks. When someone speaks, quotation marks stand ready to grasp the moment by including the punctuation mark within quotation marks.

MANY BOOKS HAVE BEEN WRITTEN using the animals' point of view. Examples include Aslan the lion from *The Chronicles of Narnia* and the young mouse Matthias from the *Redwall* series.

What if animals really could talk? On your paper, list four animals. Beside each animal, write what that animal might say if finally given the chance to speak! Pay special attention to the use of punctuation marks.

EXAMPLES

Sheep: "Baa? Really? Was this the best I could get?"

Leopard: "But I'm a vegetarian!"

Cow: "Do these spots make me look fat?"

Python: "Never swallow anything larger than you are."

Ready? Take Five!

SUPPLIES
Student W.A.L.L.

STANDARDS
Demonstrate command of the conventions of standard English capitalization, punctuation, and spelling when writing

Use narrative techniques such as dialogue, pacing, and description to develop experiences, events, and/or characters

TEACHER TIP
Among the books that could be used as examples are the following:

Aesop's Fables

Alice in Wonderland

Animal Farm

Beatrix Potter tales

The Chronicles of Narnia

The Cricket in Times Square

The Jungle Book

Ralph S. Mouse

The Wind in the Willows

A cool tool students will enjoy is available at **www.fotobabble .com**. Here a photo of an animal can be uploaded and given the power of speech through the student's own voice.

LANGUAGE LINK

problem solving

LEARNING SETTING

pair

SUPPLIES
Student W.A.L.L.

STANDARDS
Present information, findings, and supporting evidence such that listeners can follow the line of reasoning and the organization, development, and style are appropriate to task, purpose, and audience

Read closely to determine what the text says explicitly and to make logical inferences from it; cite specific textual evidence when writing or speaking to support conclusions drawn from the text

TEACHER TIP
This game allows each player one turn. For future Take Fives, you can provide additional sets of mixed letters such as SLPAERNO and EEVCIRS. Once they have completed one game, they will want to do it again!

spill and spell

ALONG WITH THE GAME OF SCRABBLE, another word game is Spill and Spell, where players shake a container of letter cubes and toss them onto the table. The letters that land face up are the ones that players must use to make the largest word possible, or several smaller words if strategically placed horizontally or vertically.

If, for instance the letters "R, S, U, T, N, A" were to spill onto the table, a player might spell *Saturn* or the following combination:

S

A

T U R N

If you want to keep score, count one point for each letter used. In this game, there is no penalty for unused letters. They simply do not count. Ready? The cubes are now in the container. The shaking has begun. With a flick of the wrist, you toss the container and the letters come spilling out. Allow one minute per play.

Player One: Here are your letters: "P, A, R, E, C, T."

On your paper, use these letters to construct your words. Player Two will serve as the time keeper. When time is called, count up the points. Player Two will then begin.

Player Two: Here are your letters: "T, I, N, O, A, C."

Ready? Take Five!

story stick

A TREASURED ITEM FOR MANY NATIVE AMERICAN TRIBES was the wooden "talking stick." This ceremonial stick was decorated with beads, feathers, and designs. It was used to maintain order at council meetings and to assist in telling stories that had been passed down from one generation to another. Each design served as a story starter, bringing tales alive through the words of the gifted storyteller.

In today's task, each group will not be retelling stories. Instead, they will be creating one of their own.

The small stick before each group is a plain one without any markings. The first storyteller will hold the stick and begin the first words of a story. After this, the stick is passed to the next person who will add to the story. The story will continue to grow as it is passed around the circle. The duty of the first storyteller is to make sure the stick makes its way around the circle in a timely manner.

Just before the time limit ends, the first storyteller must bring the story to a close. Then, as a team, select a design that represents this highly unusual story. The story starter will then draw the design onto the stick using a marker.

Ready? Take Five! 5!

LANGUAGE LINK
oral traditions

LEARNING SETTING
collaboration

SUPPLIES
Small wooden dowel

STANDARDS

Use narrative techniques, such as dialogue, pacing, and description, to develop experiences, events, and/or characters

Prepare for and participate effectively in a range of conversations and collaborations with diverse partners, building on others' ideas and expressing their own clearly and persuasively

TEACHER TIP

This prompt can be repeated over and over as teams continue to add unique markings and symbols to the story stick, symbolizing each story created by the team.

Directions for making a more decorative stick can be found in the eHow article, "How to Make a Native American Talking Stick": (**www.ehow.com/ how_7380619_make-native -american-talking-stick.html**).

An extension of this lesson can be the discussion of buffalo hides as a story canvas. An interactive lesson on how to read a buffalo skin can be found at "What Story Does it Tell" page of the National Museum of American History website: **www. americanhistory.si.edu/kids/ buffalo/hideactivity**.

LANGUAGE LINK

cause-and-effect

LEARNING SETTING

individual

SUPPLIES

Student W.A.L.L.

STANDARDS

Analyze how an author's choices concerning how to structure a text, order events within it (e.g., parallel plots), and manipulate time (e.g., pacing, flashbacks) create such effects as mystery, tension, or surprise

Provide a conclusion that follows from the narrated experiences or events

TEACHER TIP

An interactive video of two young stowaways can be viewed on the ABC's website: "A Stowaway's Guide to the Pacific: an adventure in 6 parts": **www.abc.net.au/ stowaways.**

Caution: It is rather long, much like viewing a movie. Be sure to swipe the cursor over objects (such as the cave paintings) for added interest.

stowaway

AS A STOWAWAY ON A SHIP, you have managed to remain hidden from the crew. For you, this was an opportunity of a lifetime, a chance to see the world. Unfortunately, things haven't gone quite as planned.

For one thing, the ship you chose has not made any ports of call, meaning it hasn't made a single stop along the way. For two weeks, you have silently slipped through the passageways at night, returning to the cargo hold at first light when the ship comes alive with activity.

Now, however, a new danger has surfaced: a strange sickness. You feel weak and lightheaded; a rash has appeared on your arms and legs. What do you do? Remain hidden for the duration of the voyage or announce your presence so that you can seek medical attention?

On your W.A.L.L., make a list of several options. Beside each option, write a possible consequence of that action. Consider each idea carefully, and then place a star by the choice you feel would have the best outcome.

Finally, explain your decision, describing what actually happens as you provide the exposition, or outcome, of this story. Did we mention that it is pirate ship?

Ready? Take Five!

student helper 1

SO MANY PRODUCTS NOW MAKE A STUDENT'S LIFE EASIER: pencil cases for keeping writing utensils together; dividers that separate subject notes; backpacks that include special pockets for water bottles.

In front of each team is a plastic baggy containing the following items: two paperclips, one index card, a pipe cleaner, and one folder label. As a team, your challenge is to invent one item that can solve a typical problem in the classroom—one practical enough for any student to use.

Examples: a holder to keep your pencil from rolling off the desk, a need-extra-help flag to raise at your desk.

First, consider what problem this item will solve. Next, construct your new invention. Set it aside for tomorrow's challenge.

Ready? Take Five!

LANGUAGE LINK
problem solving

LEARNING SETTING
collaboration[5]

SUPPLIES

Plastic baggy with prompt materials included (can be varied)

Two paperclips

One index card

Pipe cleaner

One folder label or any adhesive-backed note

STANDARDS

Prepare for and participate effectively in a range of conversations and collaborations with diverse partners, building on others' ideas and expressing their own clearly and persuasively

Make strategic use of digital media and visual displays of data to express information and enhance understanding of presentations

Present information, findings, and supporting evidence such that listeners can follow the line of reasoning and the organization, development, and style are appropriate to task, purpose, and audience

problem solving

collaboration⁵

SUPPLIES

Plastic baggy with prompt materials included (can be varied)

Two paperclips

One index card

Pipe cleaner

One folder label or any adhesive-backed note

STANDARDS

Prepare for and participate effectively in a range of conversations and collaborations with diverse partners, building on others' ideas and expressing their own clearly and persuasively

Make strategic use of digital media and visual displays of data to express information and enhance understanding of presentations

Present information, findings, and supporting evidence such that listeners can follow the line of reasoning and the organization, development, and style are appropriate to task, purpose, and audience

TEACHER TIP

Immediate feedback can be given for each invention by using safe social networking tools such as Kidblog, a site where teachers can develop a classroom blog. See **www.kidblog.com**.

student helper 2

IT'S DEMONSTRATION TIME! Today, each team will share with the class its unique Student Helper invention. Be sure to include a clear explanation of how the product solves a common problem.

After all of the presentations have been given, hold an informal class survey or vote on the product that best meets the objective of the prompt: solving an everyday problem.

Ready? Take Five!

superhero vocabulary

THE WORDS MOST OFTEN ASSOCIATED WITH SUPERHEROES aren't words at all. They are sounds like "Kapow!," "Whack!," and "Zonk!" Today's challenge, however, is a search for real words associated with being a superhero.

Begin by writing "superhero" in the middle of a circle on your paper. Next, in typical comic book fashion, draw balloons from the center circle. In these, insert the first adjectives that come to mind, words like "smart" or "determined."

From these balloons, draw other balloons and fill them with other power words using a thesaurus. You and your partner will locate as many adjectives in the time given to discover many different and unusual words that could describe superheroes. The word *strong* might immediately come to mind, but what about *robust*, *tenacious*, or *fierce*?

Ready? Take Five!

LANGUAGE LINK

expository writing

LEARNING SETTING

individual

SUPPLIES

Student W.A.L.L.

STANDARDS

Introduce a claim(s) and organize the reasons and evidence clearly

TEACHER TIP

Students can once again enjoy creating new superhero adventures as they did in the Action Figure prompt via the Super Action Comic Maker website: **www.artisancam .org.uk/flashapps/ superactioncomicmaker.**

super powers

ALMOST EVERYONE LOVES A SUPERHERO— Captain America, Wonder Woman, Superman, Wolverine, the Invisible Woman, etc.

These characters have special powers that help them combat evil forces. One hero might have super strength; another might have the ability to stretch himself into all kinds of shapes; yet another might have the ability to walk through walls or become a ball of fire.

Imagine your surprise this morning when you awoke to find that you also have a special power. The task for today is to decide what super-power you now possess and how it will be used.

Briefly describe the super power and then explain at least three ways that it can be used.

Ready? Take Five!

super star

A STAR PLACED BESIDE SOMEONE'S NAME indicates that he or she has done something particularly well. Today, you will be a star. On your paper, draw a star. In the middle of the star, write a brief summary of something that you did really well this week. Maybe you helped someone or said something nice to someone. Now, draw a larger star outside of the first one. In the area between the two stars, describe what you would like to do next week that could make you a *super* star!

Ready? Take Five! **5!**

LANGUAGE LINK

reflective writing

LEARNING SETTING

individual

SUPPLIES

Paper

Scissors

Markers

STANDARDS

Use precise words and phrases, relevant descriptive details, and sensory language to convey experiences and events

Include multimedia components (e.g., graphics, images, music, sound) and visual displays in presentations to clarify information

SUPPLIES
Student W.A.L.L.

STANDARDS

Demonstrate understanding of figurative language, word relationships, and nuances in word meanings

Use precise words and phrases, relevant descriptive details, and sensory language to convey experiences and events

Write narratives to develop real or imagined experiences or events using effective technique, well-chosen details and well-structured event sequences

TEACHER TIP

A fun review of major literary devices can be found on the "Figures of Speech" page available through the Quia website: **www.quia.com/ hm/80390.html**. Here, students test their ability to recognize specific devices while enjoying a game of "hangman" at the same time.

tale of the tweebles

SHORT STORIES CAN COME IN ALL SHAPES AND SIZES. One unusual type is a short story where, throughout the entire tale, groups of words all begin with the same consonant sound. This is why this story is an alliterative short story. Alliteration is a literary device that involves the repetition of consonant sounds at the beginning of words. It helps lend a musical quality to writing: solitary sailor, weeping willow, or the Wailing Wall.

Your task is to see how far you can take the following story in the five-minute time limit. Remember to keep it alliterative! For example, after a series of words that begin with G, switch to the T's, L's, or some other consonant. The story begins!

EXAMPLE

Tiny Tweebles live in the damp, dense rainforest. At night, they nestle at the base of big banyan trees. At the first feeble rays of sunrise, they stir, leaping leaf to leaf, to find food. Creeping through the cover of the forest's canopy, they sense sudden strange stirrings. Stopping in their steps, they tremble, terrified . . .

Ready? Take Five!

teacher code of conduct

YEARS AGO, TEACHERS HAD TO FOLLOW A VERY STRICT CODE of behavior. In the late 1800's, many districts required them to remain single, attend church regularly, and abide by a curfew. By the 1950's, these rules had been greatly relaxed, though many female teachers were still not allowed to teach if expecting a child—even if they were married. Much has changed in the last fifty years!

If there were a code of conduct for the twenty-first century teacher, what might be included in the rules?

EXAMPLES

All teachers must whistle for first minute of class.

All teachers must share their lunch if dessert is included.

Now it's your turn. List five rules for teachers.

Ready? Take Five!

LANGUAGE LINK

expository writing

LEARNING SETTING

individual

SUPPLIES
Student W.A.L.L.

STANDARDS
Write informative/explanatory texts to examine and convey complex ideas and information clearly and accurately through the effective selections, organization, and analysis of content

TEACHER TIP
Students will enjoy seeing a list of the 1915 Rules for Teachers. These can be viewed on the "Rules for Teachers" page available through Teacherworld. com: **www.teacherworld.com/ potrules.html**

expository writing

individual

SUPPLIES

Student w.a.l.l.

STANDARDS

Write informative/explanatory texts to examine and convey complex ideas and information clearly and accurately through the effective selection, organization, and analysis of content

Use precise language and domain-specific vocabulary to inform about or explain the topic

teacher dress code

MORE AND MORE SCHOOLS ARE REQUIRING A DRESS CODE for students. This code describes the particular types of clothes and accessories students can or cannot wear. But what about teachers?

That's your job. You have been assigned the task of writing the "Dress Code for Teachers" to be included in the school handbook.

First, compile a list of five items that *can* be worn (e.g., polka-dot shirts) and then five items that should *never* be worn (e.g., makeup). As always, have fun, but be nice!

Ready? Take Five! 5!

texting haiku style

A simple yet effective form of expression is the haiku poem. Haiku builds on a series of images. Traditional haiku is created by a pattern of syllables: five syllables in the first line, seven syllables in the second line, and five syllables in the third line (a 5-7-5 pattern).

THE STRANGEST LIGHTNING STORM STRUCK LAST NIGHT. Microchips in computers and cell phones all underwent a major change. No one can quite explain it. Now, whenever someone sends an e-mail or a text, it always appears in haiku form.

EXAMPLE:

Up by two touchdowns (5)

Falcons soaring but Rams tough (7)

Stadium buzzing (5)

Your task is to write a text to one of your friends using the haiku format. Be sure to include imagery!

Ready? Take Five! 5!

LANGUAGE LINK

figurative language

LEARNING SETTING

individual

SUPPLIES

Student W.A.L.L.

STANDARDS

Write narratives to develop real or imagined experiences or events using effective techniques, well-chosen details, and well-structured event sequence

Demonstrate understanding of figurative language, word relationships, and nuances in word meanings

thar she blows!

HYPERBOLE TAKES A SITUATION, INDIVIDUAL, OR ACTION and stretches reality. It's when the fish that got away suddenly becomes "*this* big!" It's being so hungry you could eat a horse. It's a steak so tough you have to cut it with a machete. Hyperbole takes reality and stretches the truth.

In today's prompt, you are on an Alaskan cruise when suddenly you witness a profound event: a whale sighting. From the water, it slowly begins to emerge until the full length of the mammal is visible. For a fleeting moment, it seems to stand upright before its tail flips overhead as if waving goodbye. A thunderous splash marks its departure. Suddenly, all is over. The spell is broken. Recovering from your astonishment, you cannot wait to tell your friends about this event.

That's when the story begins to grow and grow and grow, stretching like the whale itself. In retelling, one whale becomes an entire pod, the cruise ship itself was in danger . . .

Stretch your imagination as you write a brief letter to a friend describing what you have just witnessed.

Ready? Take Five! 5!

that's novel

IS IT POSSIBLE TO WRITE A COMPLETE WORK OF FICTION in just one sentence? It is, according to the famous American writer Ernest Hemingway, who felt the following six words represented his best work: "For sale: baby shoes, never worn."

Another short novel was written by Guatemalan author Augusto Monterroso: "When he awoke, the dinosaur was still there." Comic book writer Howard Chaykin supplied his own approach to the single sentence novel: "I couldn't believe she'd shoot me."

Now it's your turn. Create your own exciting six-word novel that suggests to the reader far more than just those six words. Let these few words evoke images and a plot without anything more being said.

Ready? Take Five!

SUPPLIES
Student W.A.L.L.

STANDARDS
Determine a theme or central idea of a text and analyze its development over the course of the text; provide an objective summary of the text

Analyze the structure of texts, including how specific sentences, paragraphs, and larger portions of the text (e.g., a section, chapter, scene, or stanza) relate to each other and the whole

LANGUAGE LINK
cause-and-effect

LEARNING SETTING
individual

SUPPLIES
Student W.A.L.L.

STANDARDS
Use appropriate transitions to clarify the relationships among ideas and concepts

Introduce a topic; organize ideas, concepts, and information, using strategies such as definition, classification, comparison/contrast, and cause/effect; include formatting (e.g., headings), graphics (e.g., charts, tables), and multimedia when useful to aiding comprehension

they all fall down

WHEN YOU TOUCH A DOMINO, IT FALLS BACKWARD onto another domino. That domino then falls onto the next domino, and so on. The phrase "domino effect" is now used to describe a series of events that lead from one action to another.

For instance, suppose Ned has enjoyed a nice meal at an outdoor café. He stands to leave just as a person at a nearby table tosses his banana peel on the ground. As soon as Ned's shoe steps on the peel, he slips, causing his arm to hit a plate of fries a waiter is carrying.

The fries fly into the air then come raining back down, covering Rob, sitting nearby, in ketchup. His mother, Caitlin, looks up to see her son covered in "blood" and starts screaming uncontrollably. Her screams frighten Lady, who is walking along the sidewalk with her owner. Lady takes off, dragging Erin, her helpless owner, along.

Rounding the corner, they collide with Brandon on his skateboard. The skateboard sails across the street hitting a ladder, which topples to the ground leaving Jeffry dangling from the edge of the roof he was repairing.

The ladder strikes a metal trashcan that begins rolling down the street, causing two joggers to try to outrun the can . . . and so the domino effect goes.

See where you can go with the domino effect. Begin with one simple action and develop a series of causes and effects.

Ready? Take Five! 5!

time machine

WHAT IF TIME COULD STAND STILL for at least an hour, or maybe even a day or two? Imagine a remote control that works the same way as your television's remote control pause button.

Well, almost! One push of a button and you can stop time, remaining right where you are for two hours. What would that moment be? Would you be in your seat at the top of a roller coaster or playing a championship baseball game?

Describe where you are and what you are doing.

Ready? Take Five!

LANGUAGE LINK
reflective writing

LEARNING SETTING
individual

SUPPLIES
Student W.A.L.L.

STANDARDS
Produce clear and coherent writing in which the development, organization, and style are appropriate to task, purpose and audience

Use precise words and phrases, relevant descriptive details, and sensory language to convey experiences and events

LANGUAGE LINK
problem

LEARNING SETTING
individual

SUPPLIES
Student W.A.L.L.

STANDARDS
Read closely to determine what the text says explicitly and to make logical inferences from it; cite specific textual evidence when writing or speaking to support conclusions drawn from the text

Determine central ideas or themes of a text and analyze their development; summarize the key supporting details and ideas

Write narratives to develop real or imagined experiences or events using effective technique, well-chosen details, and well-structured event sequences

title terror

IT IS BOOK REPORT TIME AGAIN, and guess who isn't prepared? According to the teacher's assignment, students must select one of the following books: *To Kill a Mockingbird, The Book Thief, Lord of the Flies, The Chocolate War, The Hunger Games, Looking for Alaska,* or *Stargirl.*

Now it's time to write the summary of the book. Quickly, you scan the list. You don't have a clue about any of them. Submitting a blank sheet of paper will get you a zero for sure. There seems to be no other choice—just charge forward and hope the teacher is so overloaded that he doesn't read your paper too closely.

The task: Select one of the above titles and write a summary based on it alone. In other words, describe the plot based on a literal interpretation of the title.

For instance, instead of a story about two friends who work on a ranch in *Of Mice and Men,* the plot could be about an army of mice who poison the world supply of cheese . . . get the idea?

Ready? Take Five!

to be or not to be

SOME THINGS CAN BE DEFINED IN TERMS OF WHAT THEY *ARE*. Other things are better described by what they are *not*.

For instance, a sonnet is not random in form; a sonnet is not free writing; a sonnet is not random in length; a sonnet is not always about love; a sonnet is not without meter.

For today's task, select one word from each list and define them in terms of what they are not. Include at least four definitions for each.

List I: plot, poem, verb, semicolon

List II: pumpkin, mammal, chicken, cake, oyster

Ready? Take Five!

LANGUAGE LINK
definition

LEARNING SETTING
individual[5]

SUPPLIES
Student W.A.L.L.

STANDARDS
Develop the topic with relevant facts, definitions, concrete details, quotations, or other information and examples.

Read closely to determine what the text says explicitly and to make logical inferences from it; cite specific textual evidence when writing or speaking to support conclusions drawn from the text

TEACHER TIP
More information on sonnets, along with examples, can be found on the "Basic Sonnet Forms" page of Sonnet Central: **www.sonnets.org/basicforms .htm**

SUPPLIES
An assortment of various magazines

Glue

Tape

Plain paper

STANDARDS
Demonstrate understanding of figurative language, word relationships, and nuances in word meanings

Interpret information presented in diverse media and formats (e.g., visually, quantitatively, orally) and explain how it contributes to a topic, text, or issue under study

Integrate information presented in different media or formats (e.g., visually, quantitatively) as well as in words to develop a coherent understanding of a topic or issue

Assess how point of view or purpose shapes the content and style of a text

TEACHER TIP
This activity can be completed using a variety of magazines donated by fellow teachers or friends.

A different option is creating an interactive poster online, such as a "Glog" (**www.edu.glogster .com**) or a mosaic of images using "Mosaic Maker" at BigHugeLabs. com (**www.bighugelabs.com/ mosaic.php**).

tone it up

TWO MAGAZINES ARE ON THE TABLE IN THE DOCTOR'S OFFICE. Flipping through one of them, you read these phrases: "Enjoy the sunset," "Watercolor memories," and "Live your dreams."

Tired of that one, you pick up the second magazine. This time, you encounter some very different phrases: "Portrait of a killer," "Raise your game," and "Rugged and reliable."

Notice the difference? The first set is from a magazine designed for those who enjoy visiting exotic places while the second set is from a magazine geared for those who enjoy hunting and the rugged outdoors.

In this task, teams will be creating collages. Each team will select one audience. Examples: teenagers, science enthusiasts, fashionistas, gamers.

Next, use the magazines to tear out phrases, words, and pictures that might reflect the interests and lifestyles of the selected audience. All items will then be pasted onto one sheet of paper. When finished, all sheets will be taped together to make one large poster.

Ready? Take Five! 5!

tv guide

TV GUIDE IS A MAGAZINE THAT LISTS all television programs for the week. Your family, however, likes to create its own viewing guide by recording everyone's favorite programs.

Select any member of your family. Compile a list of television programs that would *best* characterize that person. Be careful not to include just those that he or she enjoys viewing. Selections should reflect the life and personality of that one individual.

For example: *Golf Central,* reruns of *The Andy Griffith Show, Grey's Anatomy,* and *30 Minute Meals with Rachael Ray* could represent a working mom who is employed as a nurse. She prefers spending more time on the golf course than in the kitchen, and she is a bit old fashioned.

Ready? Take Five!

SUPPLIES

Student W.A.L.L.

STANDARDS

Interpret words and phrases as they are used in a text, including determining technical, connotative, and figurative meanings, and analyze how specific word choices shape meaning or tone

Use narrative techniques, such as dialogue, pacing, and description, to develop experiences, events, and/or characters

TEACHER TIP

This prompt can be used in a variety of ways. For example:

- Summarize a book in 140 characters
- Summarize a poem in 20 characters
- Summarize nonfiction essay in 100 characters

Teachers can also create a classroom micro-blog (like Twitter) at Twiducate (**www. twiducate.com**), which is designed especially for educators and students.

twitter bug

MANY PEOPLE HAVE BEEN BITTEN BY THE TWITTER BUG. Instead of calling one person, you can now tweet your message to thousands of people on Twitter (**www .twitter.com**).

Many celebrities like to "tweet" to their fans, sending 140-character messages about their day-to-day thoughts and activities. Consider any fictional character or author from the past or present. If he or she could use this website, what message might be sent?

Select three individuals. Write a brief tweet to his or her fans. Each message must be relevant to who they are, what they might be doing, or who they might see.

EXAMPLES

Spider-Man: Stuck again . . .

Shel Silverstein: Sidewalk just ended.

Winnie the Pooh: Help! In a sticky situation.

Ready? Take Five!

uncle bill's will

YOUR FAVORITE UNCLE, UNCLE BILL, has remembered you in his will. According to his lawyer, you now own 100 acres of land. Along with the land comes enough money for developing it.

The main clause in the will, however, requires that whatever is built there cannot be for your personal pleasure or gain. So what will it be? A hospital for injured eagles? A camp for kids with a particular disease? The possibilities are endless. Today's task is to plan how this land will be developed so that it meets the condition of the will.

First, provide the name of the project. Next, explain the purpose of the project. Be sure to include who or what will benefit from the project. Finally, provide a description of the project.

Create a graphic organizer to break down the three parts of this prompt. You may use one like the example provided, or you can create one of your own.

SUPPLIES
Student W.A.L.L.

STANDARDS

Introduce claim(s) and organize the reasons and evidence clearly

Develop the topic with relevant facts, definitions, concrete details, quotations, or other information and examples

TEACHER TIP

Another option for this prompt is the brainstorming website bubbl.us (**www.bubbl.us**) where students can create their own graphic organizers.

Ready? Take Five! 5!

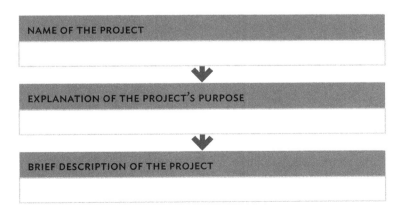

NAME OF THE PROJECT

EXPLANATION OF THE PROJECT'S PURPOSE

BRIEF DESCRIPTION OF THE PROJECT

LANGUAGE LINK

words and phrases

LEARNING SETTING

individual

SUPPLIES
Student W.A.L.L.

STANDARDS
Determine or clarify the meaning of unknown and multiple-meaning words and phrases by using context clues, analyzing meaningful word parts, and consulting general and specialized reference materials, as appropriate

Develop the topic with relevant facts, definitions, concrete details, quotations, or other information and examples

TEACHER TIP
Students will enjoy creating compound words with the online compound word games compiled at: **www. languageartsgames.4you4free .com/compound_words.html**.

Another variation of the prompt is to provide a stack of note cards with a different base word on each. Give each student one card. Students can then challenge themselves to match their base word with another to form a compound word. After each compound word is created, it can then be added to a growing list for all the class to see. Warning: it can be a bit chaotic, but fun! A list of base words can be found at the above website.

undertow

Words that are joined together become known as compound words. **Closed compound** *words simply hook together (e.g., boxcar, firefly).* **Hyphenated compound** *words use a hyphen to join them together (e.g., mother-in-law, sixteen-year-old).* **Open compounds** *are neither hyphenated nor hook; they simply bump together then part slightly (e.g., half moon, credit card).*

UNDERWEAR, UNDERESTIMATE, UNDERTOW—these compound words all have one thing in common. Their meanings all stem from being "below" in some way.

An "underdog," for instance, is a competitor who is below the favored one. The "undertow" is a strong current that runs below the surface of the water and can be dangerous for swimmers. If you "underestimate" the importance of a test and barely study, you might be surprised at the results. As for "underwear," well, that one is rather obvious.

Now consider the opposite of "under." How many *original* compound words can you list that begin with the word "over," meaning "beyond"? How about "over-homework" (homework that is piled on top of other homework)? Create five new words and write your own definition beside each one.

Ready? Take Five!

underwater theme park

SPONGEBOB SQUAREPANTS AND ALL HIS FRIENDS are so excited! They are going on a vacation to an underwater theme park. Two of you are going along to take pictures. At the end of the day, you will look back through hundreds of photographs and select five pictures to print and label using active verbs.

FOR EXAMPLE

Picture #1

Mr. Krabs **growls** *at the camera as he emerges from the Seagrass Maze.*

Picture #2

SpongeBob **slurps** *down a sixteen-ounce Frozen Algae Foam.*

Picture #3

Patrick Star **races** *to the finish line in the Seahorse Race.*

Maybe you aren't that familiar with this cast of characters. Select any group of common characters and place them in a theme park. Next, describe five photographs using active verbs.

Be sure to identify the individuals in each photo as well as the activity taking place.

Ready? Take Five!

LANGUAGE LINK

parts of speech

LEARNING SETTING

pair

SUPPLIES
Student W.A.L.L.

STANDARDS
Demonstrate command of the conventions of standard English grammar and usage when writing or speaking

Form and use verbs in the active and passive voice

Analyze how particular lines of dialogue or incidents in a story or drama propel the action, reveal aspects of a character, or provoke a decision

Use precise words and phrases, relevant descriptive details, and sensory language to convey experiences and events

TEACHER TIP
As an extension to this Take Five, students can create their own digital avatars using Voki at **www.yoki.com**. Best of all, the labels developed for this prompt can be spoken by the characters using the students' voices, or they can type the labels and select the voices they want to describe the scene.

expository writing

individual

SUPPLIES

Student W.A.L.L.

STANDARDS

Draw evidence from literary or informational texts to support analysis, reflection, and research

Introduce claim(s) and organize the reasons and evidence clearly

Develop the topic with relevant facts, definitions, concrete details, quotations, or other information and examples

up, up, and away

TINKER BELL CAN DO IT. SO COULD DUMBO, IRON MAN, and Superman. What do they have in common? They can all fly! Imagine if you could spread your arms (or ears!) and swoop into the sky. Where would you go and what would you want to do or see?

Make a list of five unique things you would do if you could fly.

Ready? Take Five!

vanity tag

VANITY TAGS (PERSONALIZED LICENSE PLATES) HAVE CREATED a new game for the road that is even better than counting the number of green, yellow, or red cars that pass. In this game, travelers must decipher the "code," to discover the true message on a car tag.

Some are easier to "decode" than others. DEBUG could belong to an exterminating company; LWR8S (lower rates) could be the brainchild of a mortgage company. An accountant might use ADUMUP (ad um up) and a barbecue restaurant owner might enjoy HOLHOG (whole hog).

The task today is to create two vanity tags. One might be for a business, the other for a sports team or maybe a favorite hobby. No more than seven characters may be used. A license plate template is provided for you to copy.

RU RDY? Take Five!

LANGUAGE LINK

parts of speech

LEARNING SETTING

pair

SUPPLIES
Student W.A.L.L.

STANDARDS
Determine or clarify the meaning of unknown and multiple-meaning words and phrases by using context clues, analyzing meaningful word parts, and consulting general and specialized reference materials, as appropriate

Demonstrate command of the conventions of standard English grammar and usage when writing or speaking

Distinguish among the connotations (associations) of words with similar denotations (definitions) (e.g., stingy, scrimpy, economical, thrifty)

Prepare for and participate effectively in a range of conversations and collaborations with diverse partners, building on others' ideas and expressing their own clearly and persuasively

vocabulary for villains

VILLAINS HAVE THEIR OWN UNIQUE CHARACTERISTICS. Words usually associated with villains are tricky, evil, rude, angry, and greedy.

Pair up for this diabolical challenge. Then, write and circle the word "villain" in the middle of your W.A.L.L. Next, draw comic balloons from the circle to capture the most villainous adjectives you can think of.

Work with a thesaurus to discover a new way to say evil, greedy, or tricky.

Ready? Take Five!

vowel art

AT THE TOP OF YOUR PAPER, COPY THE FOLLOWING VOWELS: A, E, I, O, U, Y. Next, move your pencil to the middle of your sheet of paper. Now, work with each vowel, rotating and moving them around until you have created the base for a picture that you will draw.

All vowels must be used in the overall picture, connecting as many vowels you can. For instance, by turning the "E" on its back and then placing the "A" on top, you begin the base for a structure. Make sure all vowels appear in bold color. Use your imagination to complete the overall scene.

Ready? Take Five!

LANGUAGE LINK

vowels

LEARNING SETTING

individual

SUPPLIES

Student W.A.L.L.

Plain paper

Markers

Colored pencils

Computer Paint or Draw tools (opt.)

STANDARDS

Make strategic use of digital media and visual displays of data to express information and enhance understanding of presentations

TEACHER TIP

This prompt can be accomplished online by using the ReadThinkWrite Webbing Tool: **http://interactives.mped.org/ webbing127.aspx**

SUPPLIES
Student W.A.L.L.

Markers or colored pencils

STANDARDS
Produce clear and coherent writing in which the development, organization, and style are appropriate to task, purpose, and audience

Demonstrate understanding of figurative language, word relationships, and nuances in word meanings

Make strategic use of digital media and visual displays of data to express information and enhance understanding of presentations

TEACHER TIP
After the students have completed this prompt, they can generate discussion and awareness of their favorite causes by wearing their ribbons around school. If ribbon assortment is available, students could use their prototype to create an actual ribbon for their campaign. Ribbons could also be displayed in the classroom.

Colorful templates and examples are also available on Wikipedia's Awareness Ribbon page: **www.en.wikipedia.org/wiki/ Awareness_ribbon**

wear a ribbon

PINK RIBBON SUPPORTERS FIGHT BREAST CANCER; red ribbon wearers say no to drugs. But what about brown ribbons with green polka dots or emerald ribbons with wavy white lines? What do they mean?

In the brown and green example, the ribbon could support local farmers. Brown would represent the dirt of the farm and the green dots would represent the green plants that grow from the rich soil. The emerald ribbons could represent the gulf waters in a "Protect our beaches" campaign.

In this task, select an original campaign or cause. Next, design a ribbon and provide a slogan to appear on it.

Ready? Take Five!

western drawl

THE YEAR IS 1873. JESSE JAMES AND HIS MEN have been blazing a trail of crime as they rob banks, trains, and stagecoaches. You are riding one of those trains that has suddenly been stopped in its tracks by the famous James gang.

All is quiet as the men slip from their horses, guns drawn, and approach the train. The engineer is helpless to move the train due to the blockade of downed trees on the tracks, a perfect ambush. As the rough outlaws climb aboard, angry voices and frightened cries suddenly come alive. One deadly look from their leader and all is quiet once again. No one knows what to expect.

Finally, Jesse and his brother Frank look around and speak. Their words take everyone by complete surprise! The brothers' tough Western dialect has been replaced with today's modern slang. In this task, you are to write a short dialogue featuring Jesse, Frank, and the train conductor. Are you ready for this challenge, partner . . . ah, I mean dude? Remember—there are women and children on this train, so keep it clean.

Ready, aim . . . Take Five!

LANGUAGE LINK

words and phrases

LEARNING SETTING

individual

SUPPLIES
Student W.A.L.L.

STANDARDS
Write narratives to develop real or imagined experiences or events using effective technique, well-chosen details, and well-structured event sequences

Determine the meaning of words and phrases as they are used in the text, including figurative and connotative meanings; analyze the cumulative impact of specific word choices on meaning and tone (e.g., how the language evokes a sense of time and place; how it sets a formal or informal tone)

SUPPLIES
Student W.A.L.L.

STANDARDS
Write informative/explanatory texts to examine and convey complex ideas and information clearly and accurately through the effective selection, organization, and analysis of content

Develop the topic with relevant facts, definition, concrete details, or other information and examples

Use appropriate transitions to create cohesion and clarify the relationships among ideas and concepts

TEACHER TIP
Students can enjoy an extension to this prompt by creating their own special brews by mixing lemonade, fruit juices, carbonated water, and other real-world ingredients.

what's in your brew?

WITCHES AND WIZARDS ALWAYS SEEM TO HAVE something brewing. From their black pots, a variety of strange smells and vapors linger. Slowly, they stir and toss in each ingredient—horned toads, knotgrass, nettles, spiders, and bat wings.

Potions could do many things: inspire love, extend life, heal illnesses, cause pain, erase memory, or cause blindness. The three witches in Shakespeare's play *Macbeth* predicted future events through their potent mixture. Merlin, a legendary wizard, is considered a master of potions and spells in the legend of King Arthur.

In today's prompt, you will develop your own potion. On your W.A.L.L., give the potion a name, list the ingredients, and describe how to make it. Be sure to describe the purpose for the potion.

Ready? Take Five! 5!

wild goose chase

YOU'VE JUST ARRIVED IN AMERICA FROM ANOTHER COUNTRY. You feel comfortable talking with Americans because you've studied the English language for many years. But something's not right! You just overheard that someone had "gone haywire" and someone else was described as being a "couch potato." Weird images begin forming in your head. A couch made of potatoes? How can that be?

Welcome to the world of idioms, figurative expressions that have a different meaning than the literal meaning of the words. For example, maybe you know someone who has "jumped the gun" or "put the cart before the horse."

In this task, you are to view the world as an outsider might see it. Select one idiom from the list provided or pick your own. Draw the image of the idiom as it might seem to appear in literal terms. Write the idiom above the image.

Idioms:		
bull-headed	lend a hand	blue in the face
pretty penny	on the dot	under the weather
out of hand	up the creek	kick the bucket
catch a bite	pull someone's leg	wild goose chase
hit the books	rub the wrong way	top dog
ditch school	shoot the breeze	chicken out
over one's head	sleep on it	smell a rat
jump the gun	tightwad	eat crow

Get the picture? Then don't waste another minute.

Ready? Take Five!

problem
LANGUAGE LINK

LEARNING SETTING

individual

SUPPLIES
Paper strips

Markers

Computer Paint or Draw software (opt.)

STANDARDS
Cite several pieces of textual evidence to support analysis of what the text says explicitly as well as inferences drawn from the text

Apply knowledge of language to understand how language functions in different contexts, to make effective choices for meaning or style, and to comprehend more fully when reading or listening

Determine the meanings of words and phrases as they are used in text, including figurative and connotative meanings; analyze the impact of a specific word choice on meaning and tone

---

TEACHER TIP
A more complete list of common idioms can be found by visiting the Idiom Site at **www. idiomsite.com**.

Or, check out the "English Idioms and Quizzes" page of the Idiom Connection website: **www. idiomconnection.com**.

descriptive writing

individual

SUPPLIES

Student W.A.L.L.

STANDARDS

Use precise words and phrases, relevant descriptive details, and sensory language to convey experiences and events

Use narrative techniques, such as dialogue, pacing, and description, to develop experiences, events, and/or characters

wild thing

IF YOU HAVE EVER VISITED A ZOO, you have probably seen monkeys, lions, snakes, and maybe even a zebra or elephant. There's one animal, however, that you haven't seen–in fact, no one has. On your W.A.L.L., draw two small circles, one on top of the other, then complete the rest of the animal with your own imagination. Your animal must be unique, one that no one has even seen before.

Give your animal a name and then write a lively description of your creation that includes its habitat, eating habits, and other special characteristics.

Ready? Take Five! 5!

word game

HERE'S AN EASY WORD GAME FOR TODAY'S TASK. After selecting a word from the list (or one of your own), begin the following sequence: Take away a letter to form a new word. Next, change one letter to form a new word. Continue in this sequence until no new word can be created.

EXAMPLE:

Bread

Take away a letter = ***bead***

Change a letter = ***beam***

Take away a letter = ***bam***

Change a letter = ***ram***

Take away a letter = ***am***

Change a letter = ***as***

Take away a letter = ***a***

The objective is to arrive at the very smallest unit of letters that still makes a word.

Word List: cloud, trace, tiger, feather, travel, blade, harsh

Remember that you can move the letters around after a letter has been dropped. Got your pencil handy?

Ready? Take Five!

SUPPLIES
Student W.A.L.L.

STANDARDS
Introduce a topic: organize ideas, concepts, and information, using strategies such as definition, classification, comparison/contrast, and cause-and-effect; include formatting (e.g., headings), graphics (e.g., charts, tables), and multimedia when useful to aiding comprehension

Read closely to determine what the text says explicitly and to make logical inferences from it; cite specific textual evidence when writing or speaking to support conclusions drawn from the text

Use a variety of techniques to sequence events so that they build on one another to create a coherent whole

TEACHER TIP
Another example for students is the word chair. This provides an example of how far the game can be taken without reaching the final objective: a one-letter word.

Take away a letter = hair
Change a letter = lair
Take away a letter = air
Change a letter = aid
Take away a letter = ad
Change a letter = id
Take away a letter= I

SUPPLIES
Student W.A.L.L.

STANDARDS
Write informative/explanatory texts to examine a topic and convey ideas, concepts, and information through the selection, organization, and analysis of relevant content

Use appropriate transitions to clarify the relationships among ideas and concepts

TEACHER TIP
Other comparisons that can be made include the following:

Learning to swim
Hunting a deer
Organizing a party
Baking a pizza
Playing a sport

writing is like . . .

FISHING IS LIKE WRITING AN ESSAY. First, you must hook your catch. Like the fish, you want to catch as many different topics as possible. Next is the selection process. Which one will you choose? For this, you must know your limits. In Florida, a saltwater trout must be at least fifteen inches in length to keep. A redfish must be between eighteen and twenty-seven inches in length.

In the same way, an essay topic needs to be big enough to be covered within the required limit, but not so small that it can't be stretched to the required length. Catching it is one thing, but you still have to haul it into the boat. Strain those muscles. Use everything you've got to get your catch into the boat. This is like drafting, where you give all you've got to write down every idea related to the topic.

After this, it's time to clean your catch; this is where the editing process comes in. You have to decide what stays and what goes. Cooking your fish is the same as writing the final copy. The best part of this whole process is now about to begin—yum! Taste it, read it, share it with others. The task today is to write a paragraph comparing the process of writing to some other activity. What about shopping or taking a vacation? Think of many different ideas before tackling this task.

Ready? Take Five! 5!

yellow brick roadblock

LANGUAGE LINK
problem

LEARNING SETTING
individual

SUPPLIES
Student W.A.L.L.

STANDARDS
Introduce claim(s) and organize the reasons and evidence clearly

Assess how point of view or purpose shapes the content and style of a text

HARD TIMES HAVE HIT MGM, THE FAMOUS MOVIE STUDIO. They must make some major cutbacks or they will close at the end of the year. The story of a wizard called Oz and a place called Emerald City was supposed to be one of its biggest hits ever! Now, even this tale of Dorothy and her dog Toto is on the chopping block.

The producers have decided that twenty minutes will need to be cut from the final film. Victor Fleming, the director, has gone through each frame trying his best to decide what must go. Finally, with the help of his film editor, he has made a decision. One of Dorothy's guides along the Yellow Brick Road must be cut. That's right— the Cowardly Lion, the heartless Tin Man, or the brainless Scarecrow. But who will it be?

As the film editor, you must make the decision. Who will be going and why? In making your decision, consider the following factors:

Which character will have the least impact on the outcome of the story?

Which character will audiences enjoy more?

Which character may become a profitable marketing tool, particularly for a fast food chain that caters to young children?

In a paragraph, develop your most convincing argument.

Ready? Take Five! 5!

descriptive writing

pair

SUPPLIES

Student W.A.L.L.

STANDARDS

Demonstrate understanding of figurative language, word relationships, and nuances in word meanings

Distinguish among the connotations (association) of words with similar denotations (definitions) (e.g., stingy, scrimpy, economical, unwasteful, thrifty)

Consult reference materials (e.g., dictionaries, glossaries, thesauruses), both print and digital, to find the pronunciation of a word or determine or clarify its precise meaning or its part of speech

yucky café 1

MAKE A VISIT TO THE YUCKY CAFÉ, LOCATED IN GROSS OUT, Nevada. The Yuck (as locals like to call it) serves very unusual foods to its customers. You can't be squeamish here. It's always a taste bud adventure.

Recent hits have included toasted black pepper beetle shells, steamed lemony caterpillars, and sweet egg slushies. The café has become so popular that it now needs a menu. Use a thesaurus to pull out your best adjectives to describe the foods and drink that will be featured in this very unique restaurant.

Tomorrow's Take Five will take it one step farther into the world of Yuck when you will create your menu based on today's food choices.

Ready? Take Five!

yucky café 2

PULL OUT YESTERDAY'S LIST OF ITEMS for the Yuck's new menu. Today, you and a partner will combine your list and create the menu. Be sure to illustrate with eye-popping, mouth-watering designs. You might even consider a slogan or logo: "You'll be lucky when you eat at Yucky's!"

Ready? Take Five!

LANGUAGE LINK

descriptive writing

LEARNING SETTING

pair

SUPPLIES

Pens

Art supplies

Plain paper

Software program (opt.)

STANDARDS

Make strategic use of digital media and visual displays of data to express information and enhance understanding of presentations

TEACHER TIP

Examples of thematic menus can be viewed at the following websites:

The Buckhorn Exchange
www.buckhorn.com

Ye Old Tavern
www.yeoldetavern.net

The Rain Forest Café
www.rainforestcafe.com

For students who are just beginning to explore the world of paint tools, ReadWriteThink Printing Press, an online graphics program, can provide an easy introduction. The brochure option will provide the tools students will need to create their menus. Easy-to-follow buttons guide students through the creating process: **http://interactives. mped.org/ppress110.aspx**.

appendix

Language Link Cross Index

This index is a guide to the Language Link connected with each prompt. Language Links alert teachers to the skill correlated to each prompt. This index lists the Language Link (e.g., cause-and-effect, descriptive writing), the prompt, the Learning Setting (LS), and the page number. The Learning Settings include the following: Individual (I), Pair (P), and Collaborative (C). High five designations (^{5}) are used to mark the more challenging prompts.

Language Link	Prompt	LS	Page
Aphorism	Say What?	I^5	146
Audience	Tone It Up	C	178
Author's Purpose	The Next Kid/Teen Chef	I	108
Cause-and-Effect	Ban All Books	I	24
	Foggy Footsteps	I	62
	One-Eyed Mystery	I	119
	Paper or Plastic? II	I	123
	Pot of Gold	I	134
	Slithery, Slimy, Scaly	I	156
	Stowaway	I	162
	They All Fall Down	I	174
Characterization	Character Interview	I	32
	Check It Out! I	I	34
	Check It Out! II	I	35
	Clay Creatures I	P	45
	Clay Creatures II	P	46
	Invitation Only	P	83
	Junk Mail	C	84
	Missing Pet I	C	98
	Missing Pet II	C	99
	Romeo, Romeo I	I^5	142
	Romeo, Romeo II	I^5	143
	TV Guide	I	179
	Twitter Bug	I	180

Learning Setting Cross Index

On those days when a group activity is particularly needed, this Learning Setting Cross Index can help quickly locate prompts that will meet that need. Prompts are divided into the following groups: Individual, Pair, and Collaborative. High five designations (^{5}) are also included to mark those prompts that might prove more challenging than others.

Bibliography

Bruner, Jerome S. (1979). *On Knowing: Essays for the Left Hand.* 2nd ed. Cambridge, MA: Belnap Press: Harvard University Press.

Dewey, John (1998). *Experience and Education: The 60th Anniversary Edition.* Indianapolis, IN: Kappa Delta Pi.

Gardner, Howard. (1993). *Frames of Mind: The Theory of Multiple Intelligences.* New York: Basic Books.

Gardner, Howard. (2004). *The Unschooled Mind: How Children Think and How Schools Should Teach.* New York: Basic Books.

Guilford, J.P. (1967). *The Nature of Human Intelligence.* New York: McGraw-Hill.

Hendrick, Joanne and Weissman, Patricia. (1980). *The Whole Child: Developmental Education for the Early Years.* 2nd ed. St. Louis, MO: The C.V. Mosby Company.

Reis, Sally M. and Renzulli, Joseph S. (1985). *The Schoolwide Enrichment Model: A Comprehensive Plan for Educational Excellence.* Mansfield Center, CT: Creative Learning Press.

Schlichter, Carol and W. Ross Palmer, eds. (1993). *Thinking Smart: A Primer of the Talents Unlimited Model.* Mansfield Center, CT: Creative Learning Press.

Sternberg, Robert J. (1985). *Beyond IQ: A Triarchic Theory of Human Intelligence.* Cambridge: Cambridge University Press.

Taylor, Calvin W. (1968). "Be Talent Developers as Well as Knowledge Dispensers." *Today's Education: The Journal of the National Education Association,* 57, 67-69.

Taylor, Calvin W. and Barron, Frank, eds. (1963). *Scientific Creativity, its Recognition and Development: Selected Papers from the Proceedings of the First, Second, and Third University of Utah Conferences: "The Identification of Creative Scientific Talent."* Oxford, England: John Wiley.

Thurstone, Louis Leon. (1975). *Primary Mental Abilities.* Chicago: University of Chicago Press.